LOCATION OF CULTURE IN SAUL BELLOW AND I. B. SINGER :

A COMPARATIVE STATEMENT ON THE VICTIM AND SHOSHA

LOCATION OF CULTURE IN SAUL BELLOW AND I. B. SINGER :

A COMPARATIVE STATEMENT ON THE VICTIM AND SHOSHA

Dr.Pradnyashailee Bhagwan Sawai

PARTRIDGE

A Penguin Random House Company

To order additional copies of this book, contact
Partridge India
000 800 10062 62
orders.india@partridgepublishing.com

www.partridgepublishing.com/india

Contents

Acknowledgement

I am very pleased that Patridge India is publishing my first book. I thank all the people of Penguin and Patridge family. They have guided and helped me very humbly and kindly throughout the publication process. I thank my father Bhagwan Sawai and mother Subhadra Sawai because of whom I am able to face the world courageously. I am ever obliged and thankful to my soulmate, my better half, my love, Rahul Bramhane, without whom this book was simply impossible. He is a great support and encouragement for my career and life. My sons Veerbhadra and Yashodhan are a constant source of joy and happiness, they made me complete, thanks children.

Further, I am also thankful to all my teachers who taught me the art of life. I pay my gratitude to my teacher Dr.A.G.Khan, who is my M.phil and Ph.d Guide as well and who has given foreward to this book.

I would like to mention my indebtedness to the Librarian and staff of Indo - American centre for International Studies (IACIS), Osmania University, Hyderabad, and Dr. Babasaheb Ambedkar Marathwada University, Aurangabad, whose valuable co- operation helped me to acess all the required reference books. I express my thanks to IACIS and Dr. Babasaheb Ambedkar Marathwada University.

The earnest desire and constant inspiration of my sisters Padmapani and Karunasavitri, my mother- in- law

Mrs. Pramila Bramhane and father – in – law Late Sitaramji Bramhane, friends from Aurangabad and Amravati enabled me to complete this book. I wish to remain ever in their indebtedness. I am also thankful to Late Mr. P.J.Ahire who made available all the internet sources required for this book. I thank the Director, all the teaching and non – teaching staff members of Government Vidarbha Institute of Science and Humanities for their cooperation and help. Lastly I thank all the people attached to my life for their valuable contribution to enrich and strengthen my life.

Dr. Pradnyashailee BhagwanSawai
Assistant Professor, Department of English
Government Vidarbha Institute of Science and
Humanities,Amravati, Maharashtra, India

Foreword

*Ever since the end of the Cuban crisis, cultural studies have gained significant status in American and Western universities. In India however, the cultural studies programmes were somehow interlinked with interdisciplinary studies in English and vernacular literatures. Dr.Pradnyashailee Sawai decided to write a monograph on two major Jewish novels, **The Victim** by Saul Bellow and **Sosha** by Isaac Bashevis Singer. Interestingly these two prominent Jewish writers demonstrate two very different perspectives on Jewish life in America and generally in Europe after the Holocaust. While Bellow is extremely sensitive to the nuances of everyday life in USA, Singer delves deep into the traces of a bygone era.*

*In her assessment of Bellow's **The Victim,** Dr.Sawai has effectively pointed out those areas of Jewish experience that arrestingly capture the ethnic conflict between an individual and his social milieu.Asa Levanthal is constantly reminded of his Jewishness generating within him an unsettling sense of unease and restlessness. **Sosha,** on the contrary, is an anguished engagement with the past. Questions such as: Who is Shosha?Where does she come from?Where exactly is she located?become secondary in the face of a sense of colossal loss. Is she a memory?Is the memory erasable?How does a writer retrievea complex corporal experience from the baffling maze of history and time. These are the questions that are deeply* grounded in the very texture of **Sosha.** In one of the Paris Review interviews, Singer was asked; "What does the Jew suffer from?"Singer quickly replied,"The Jew may suffer from all kinds of ailments, he does not suffer from amnesia". **Sosha** is a creative embodiment of that faith.

The human soul moves perpetuallythrough various phases of time and history. It may have been physically annihilated but the spirit does not whither, it surfaces over and over again, even if in the form of a resilient memory. **The Victim** and **Shosha** are extraordinary texts,both in terms of their complex cultural locations and in their experiential texture.

While going through the draft of this book, I found that Dr.Sawai has astutely followed the norms of scholarly writing. Elaborate discussions on issues such as the Holocaust, Semitism, the Kabbalistic tradition etc. generate the necessary focus and the background against which writers like Bellow and Singer need tobe studied.

I am very happy that Dr.Sawai decided to write this com prehensive book on Bellow and Singer. I am sure it will prove to be a useful research tool for many scholars interested in pursuing their academic interest in the study of Jewish – American literature.

I wish her all the best. May her interest in this area thrive further.

Dr.A.G.Khan

This Book is dedicated to my Loving and Dear Father, my Papa, Shri.Bhagwan Shankarrao Sawai

Papa this book is for you and because of you……….

- Munna

Chapter – I

INTRODUCTION

A. The Meaning and Location of Culture:-

It is necessary to understand the meaning of culture. Culture involves artistic and other activity of the mind, a state of high development in art and thought existing in a society and represented at various level in its members, the particular system of art, thought, and customs of a society; the arts, customs, beliefs, and all the other products of human thought made by people at a particular time,; development and improvement of the mind or body by education or training.

[1]'Cult' means a group of people believing in a particular system of religious worship, with its special customs and ceremonies, worship of or loyalty to a person, principle etc, the group of people following a popular fashion or a particular interest. 'Cultivable' is a thing that can be cultivated 'cultivate' means to prepare land for growing crops, to plant, grow and raise by preparing the soil, providing, with water etc, to improve or develop by careful attention, training, or study: to cultivate a love of art to encourage the growth of friendship with or the good will of a person.

'Cultivated' means having or showing good education and manners, sensitivity etc. 'Cultivation' is the act of cultivating, to bring new land under cultivation; the state or quality of being cultivated. 'Cultivator' is a person who cultivates, a tool or machine for loosening the earth around growing plants, destroying unwanted plants etc. 'Cultural' is related to culture, culturalindependence and finally'cultured' means grown or produced by man a cultured pearl, having or showing good education, good manners, sensitivity etc.

Literature depicts the struggle of the common man. His quest for identity, struggle for existence and want of culture forms a major part of literature. There are different cultures in the world. And the writers, poets and authors have brought this culture before us through their literary creations. The suffering of common man has no boundaries. Culture has given a lot of sufferings to the ethnic groups of people worldwide. And we have to study the relation of human sufferings with culture and its representation in literature before reading any piece of literature.

"A boundary is not that at which something stops, but, as the Greeks recognized the boundary is that from which something begins its presencing".[2]
- Martin Heidegger,
"Building, dwelling, thinking",

It is the trend of our times to put the question of culture in the 'beyond'. Our existence today is marked by a tremendous sense of survival, living on the borderlines of the 'present[1] for which there seems to be no proper name other than the current and controversial shiftiness of the prefix 'post'; postomdernism, post colonialism, post feminism etc.

The 'beyond' is neither a new horizon, nor a leading behind of the Past. Beginnings and endings are the sustaining myths of the middle years. We are moving away from the differences of class' or 'gender' and are strongly moving towards differences of race, gender, generation,institutional location, geopolitical locale, sexual orientation that inhabit any claim to identity in the modern world. What is the dire need today is to think beyond narratives of of cultural differences. These 'in between' space provide the terrain for elaborating strategies of selfhood, singular or communal, that initiate new signs of identity, and innovative sites of collaboration, and contestation, in the act of defining the idea of society itself.

How are subjects formed 'in-between', or in excess of, the sum of the 'parts' of difference (usually intoned as race/class/gender, etc)? How do strategies of representation or empowerment came to be formulated in the claims of communities where despite shared histories of deprivation and discrimination, the exchange of values, meanings and may not always be collaborative and communicative, but may be profoundly conflictual and even incommensurable ?

Terms of cultural engagement are produced performatively. The representation of difference must not be read as reflection of pre-given ethnic or cultural traits set in the fixed frame of tradition. The social articulation of difference, from the minority perspective is a complicated, on -going negotiation that seeks to authorize cultural hybridities that emerge in moments of historical transformation. The recognition that tradition bestows is a partial form of identification. In reconstructing the past, it introduces other, in commensurable cultural temporalities into the invention of tradition. This process stops any immediate access to an orginary identity or a'supposed' tradition. The borderline engagements of cultural difference may as often be consensual as conflictual; they may follow our definitions of tradition and modernity; realign the customary boundaries between the private and the public, high and low; and challenge traditional expectations of development and progress.

Thus writes Renee Green, the African - Amercian artist. She reflects on the need to understand cultural difference as the production of minority identities that 'split' are estranged into themselves in the 'act' of being articulated into a collective body."

"Multiculturalism doesn't reflect the complexity of the situation as I face it daily. It requires a person to step outside of him herself to actually see what he / she is doing. I don't want to condemn well meaning people and say (like those T-shirts you can buy on the street) It's a black thing, you wouldn't understand. To me that's essentialising blackness."[3]

Social differences are not simply given to experience through an already established cultural tradition; they are the signs of the emergence of community emerged as a project at once a vision and a construction that takes us 'beyond' ourselves in order to return, in a spirit of revision and reconstruction, to the political and social conditions of the present. Even then, its still a struggle for power between various groups within ethnic groups.

If the terms of our times post-modernity, post-coloniality post-feminism has any meaning at all, it does not talk in the popular use of the 'post' to indicate a continuous flow. These terms that insistently point towards the beyond, only contain its restless and revisionary energy if they transform the present into an expanded and ex-centric site of experience and empowerment.

For the demography of the new internationalism is the history of postcolonial migration, the narratives of cultural and political diaspora, the major social displacements of peasant and aboriginal communities, the poetics of exile, the pathetic condition of political and economic refugees. . The present can no longer be simply envisaged as a break or a bonding with the past and the future, past and the future, no longer a synchronic presence; our proximate self presence our public image, comes to be revealed for its discontinuities, it's inequalities, its minorities unlike the dead hand of history that tells the beads of sequential time like a rosary seeking to establish serial, casual connections, we are now confronted with what[4] Walter Benjamin describes as the blasting of a Monadic moment from the homogenous course of history, establishing a conception of the present as' the time of the now'.

What is striking about the 'new' internationalism is that the move from the specific to the general, from the material to the metaphoric, is not a smooth passage of transition and transcendence. The 'middle passage of contemporary culture, as with slavery itself, is a process of displacement and disjunction that does not totalize experience. Increasingly, 'national[1] cultures are being produced from the perspective of disenfranchised minorities.

The borderline work of culture demands an encounter with 'newness' that is not part of the continuum of past and present. It creates a sense of the new as an insurgent act of cultural translation, such art does not merely recall the past as social cause or aesthetic precedent; it renews the past, refiguring it as contingent 'in-between' space, that innovates and interrupts the performance of the present, the 'past-present becomes part of necessity, not the nostalgia' of living.

[5]Frantz Fanon, the Martinican psychoanalyst and participant in the Algerian revolution recognizes the crucial importance, for subordinated peoples, of asserting their indigenous cultural traditions and retrieving their repressed histories. But he is far too aware of the danger of the fixity and fetishism of identities within the calcification of colonial cultures to recommend that 'roots' be struck in the celebratory romance of the past or by homogenizing the history of the present. The negating activity is, indeed the intervention of the beyond' that establishes a boundary, a bridge, where 'presencing' begins because it captures something of the estranging sense of the relocation of the home and the world - the unhomeliness that is the condition of extra territorial and cross - cultural initiations. To be unhomed is not to be homeless, nor can the 'unhomely' be easily accommodated in that familiar division of social life into private and public spheres. The unhomely moment creeps up on us stealthily as our own shadow and suddenly we find ourself with [6] Henry James's Isabel Archer, in The portrait of a lady, taking the measure of our dwelling in a

state of 'incredulous terror'. And it is at this point that the
world first shrinks for Isabel and then expands enormously.
As she struggles to survive the fathomless water, the rushing
torrents, James introduces us to the 'unhomliness' inherent
in the rite of extra territorial and cross - cultural initiation.
The recesses of the domestic space become site for history's
most intricate invasions. In that displacement, the borders
between home and world become confused; and, uncannily,
the private and the public become part of each other, forcing
upon us a vision that is as divided as it is disorienting.

Although the 'unhomely' is a paradigmatic colonial and
post-colonial condition it has a resonance that can be heard
distinctly, if erratically, in fictions that negotiate the powers
of cultural difference in a range of transhistorical sites. What
of the more complex cultural situation where 'previously'
unrecognized spiritual and intellectual needs emerge form
the imposition of "foreign" ideas, cultural representations,
and structures of power. When this is placed alongside this
idea that the cultural life of the nation is 'unconsciously' lived,
then there may be a sense in which world literature could
be an emergent, prefigurative category that is concerned
with a form of cultural dissensus and alterity, where non-
consensual terms of affiliation may be established on the
grounds of historical trauma. The study of world literature
might be the study of the way in which cultures recognize
themselves through their projections of 'otherness'. Where,
once, the transmission of national traditions was the major
theme of a world literature, perhaps we can now suggest
that transnational histories of migrants, the colonized, or
political refugees-these border and frontier conditions -may
be the terrains of world literature. The centre of such a study

would neither be the 'sovereignty' of national cultures, nor the universalism of human culture, but a focus on those "freak social and cultural displacement".

Here, we are mainly concerned about the location of culture in the writings of Jewish writers such as Saul Bellow and I. B. Singer. Saul Bellow, Bernard Malamud, Philip Roth, Tillie Olsen, Grace Palay, Cynthia Ozick, Herbert Gold, Joseph Heller, E. L. Doctorow, Stanley Elkin, Hugh Nissenson; the list of important American-Jewish fiction writers (of which this mini-list names only the most obvious) is staggering in both its variety and excellence. Indisputably, the emergence of American-Jewish fiction writers since world war II is, as Mark Shechener calls it, "a social movement that has had enormous literary consequences."

Every writer writes out of a culture. That culture may be a battleground of conflicting visions and values, and the writer may either embrace or attack his cultural heritage Saul Bellow is a modern Jewish writer who writes about modern Jew in his "The Victim" whereas I.B. Singer is an orthodox writer who writes about Holocaust and the conditions after it in his "Shosha", Jewish tradition and Jewish history, especially centuries of dispersion exile, precariousness, homelessness and powerlessness, gave rise to a distinct historical attitude toward humanity and heroes. What is glorified in yiddish life and literature is intellectual pursuit, not for its own sake, but ideally, as a route to god, a means of understanding.

Much American - Jewish literature is about the sociological and psychological dimensions of Jewish life, about being Jewish in America and focuses on the Jew as everyman -an ethnic one, but an everyman. But some of the writing has been more particular, more specifically Jewish, and has emphasized the Jewish quality by relying on Jewish roots or sources. As American- Jewish fiction insists on man's mixed nature so it walks the middle line between optimism and pessimism, complete hopeful affirmation and despair: Centuries of persecution preclude easy optimism, while hope, and faith, whether in God or in a progressive future, have kept Jews away from despair. Not only is this vision balanced and moderate its estimation of man and the future, but it is deeply suspicious of the extremes. Both nihilism and romanticism are seen as wrongheaded and dangerous. As the American-Jewish novelist most interested in ideas and cultural questions. Bellow frequently takes the temperature of the culture and prescribes medication to eliminate fever or chill.

In post world war II American - Jewish fiction, family is the crucial bond that links or chains people together. In this fiction the family is the locus of narrative and the agent of meaning. From the earliest American- Jewish literature until the most recent, the family is the heart of human life Intense family feeling is a major theme in Bellow's work. Certainly family is not always depicted positively in contemporary American Jewish fiction, but it is always central.

[7]Alfred Kazin has remarked on "the age-old Jewish belief that the only possible salvation lies in thinking well, which is thinking ones's way to the root of all creation, thinking one's way to the ultimate reason of things. The emphasis on intellect and reason pervades traditional Judaism, where knowledge of sacred texts and intellectual ability to analyze and discuss them marks of highest distinction. But in traditional Judaism the intellect is not a totally separate

sphere; it is a partner of the spirit, a means to a spiritual ideal. The extraordinary high rate of literacy and experience with its sophisticated traditions, made Jewish immigrants to this country a distinct group. This is reflected in the earliest American - Jewish fiction. Contemporary American Jewish fiction in full of intellectuals.

In American - Jewish fiction, time, history and memory define human life; makes us human. This time -drenched universe is virtually opposite the mainstream of American literature and culture. While most American literature posits the United States as a new beginning, and Eden in which every man and every women can see themselves as Adam and Eve, Jewish Memory is long and profound. For the Jewish imagination Thoreau's ecstatic perpetual dawn is a terrifying amnesia, and the linked themes of times, history, and memory pervade American- Jewish fiction. For ex. E.L. Doctorow's "The book of Daniel (1971) is about the growing historical sense and recovery of memory of the protagonist, Daniel Isaacson; and Jerome Weidman's story, "My father sits in the dark" (1934), is about an immigrant Jew's enveloping memories of his old country childhood and his native American son's incomprehension.

It is not surprising that the theme of history, memory, and time are frequently focused on the most traumatic, devastating historical experience in modern Jewish history, the Holocaust. American Jewish writers have tended to avoid evoking the Holocaust directly and to repudiate the nihilism that it implicitly suggests. Contemporary American - Jewish fiction writers who have written about the Holocaust includes Bellow in "Mr. Sammler's planet", Malamud directly in many stories and indirectly in "The fixer" (1966), Philip Roth in "The Ghost writer" (1979), and "Eli, the Fanatic" (1959), and Susan Fromberg Schaeffer in "Anya" (1974). In general, American- Jewish fiction writers have written about the Holocaust by focusing on a survivor who has come to this country. In this way, they have struggled to bring together the American reality and European event, the unprecedented post war material ease and relative psychological well being on the one hand and the most unfathomable monstrous event in Jewish history on the other.

One of the outstanding Holocaust novels, Edward Lewis Wallant's "The Pawn broker" (1961) focuses its exploration of time, memory, and history on Sol Nazerman, a Holocaust victim living in New York. Employing the Metaphor of seeing as a central organizing principle, it is about what Nazerman has seen in Europe and refuses to see in Harlem, his searing vision of the Holocaustand his current self imposed blindness, his unwillingness to see. In the fictional present Nazerman's strange glasses and deformed body are signs of how the Holocaust has maimed him, physical signs of his psychological wounds.

Sol's response to his experience has been to try to blot it out of his consciousness, not to feel or remember. That attempted amnesia and armour of feelinglessness enable him to function minimally by day. But at night, especially when the anniversary of his family's destruction arrives, he is plagued by terrible dream memories of his wife's forced sexual abasement, and his daughter's and son's inhuman deaths.

Wallant's depiction of the other Holocaust survivors in the novel is basically negative. Sol's friend Tessie is slovenly and self pitying, her aged father whining and querulous; the guilt-ridden survivor Goberman is pitiful; yet repulsive. These other survivors are decidedly unenlightened by their tragic experience; through their depiction, "The pawnbroker" clearly suggests that mere survival is not enough for wisdom or virtue. Wallant's depiction of the Sol's Members of suburban American - Jewish family is caustic, even occasionally stereotypical and unbalanced; because of their deadness to the past, their lack of memory, their historicity. They refuse to see and feel what the Holocaust was; for them American life should be endlessly cheerful, and Europe place for fancy cultural trips. Morton, the suffering would be artist, is presented with sympathy, and the new relationship with Sol at the end of the novel suggests their hopeful future. But Sol's niece is a stereo typical bubble headed Jewish American Princess;his brother in law is weak, dependent, smug and full of liberal platitude; and Sol's sister is a monster of vulgarity, willed superficiality and cruelty, who rules her husband, uses her brother, and loathes her alienated son.

The major development of the novel is Sol's awakening, caused by the self sacrificial death of his assistant Jesus Ortiz. Tnere are clear indications that this awakening will enable him to function an as emotionally responsible human being; his going to mourn her father's death with Tessie is one sign. And the awakening that affects the present and future rests on a change in his attitudes towards the past, an accommodation of all the tragic suffering, and acceptance of past events.

B. Holocaust:

Just how decisive America's involvement in the Holocaust was can be distilled from a single episode in 1945. Standing about a pit containing the remains, of countless death camp victims, [8] General D. Wight D. Eisenhower directed his troops to scrutinize the destruction and the death all around. The 'starvation, cruelty and bestiality were so over powering as to leave me a bit sick". It later recalled. But Eisenhower insisted on seeing the worst the camp had to offer, and he urged the American government to send reporters and congressman because he wanted to "leave no room for cynical doubt".

Everything significant in American relationship to Holocaust was symbolized in that scene;

1. The Mandate to remember and the resistance to remembering and

2. The deep impression that the Holocaust would make on American (and American Jewish) life and culture. Americans are not eager to absorb the historical impact of the Holocaust. The reason may be obvious, its central horror is simply too shocking to grasp Americans are certainly not alone in this respect, but they have devised unique defenses against discussing the subject. Above all is the assertion that the Holocaust occurred on a different continent and in the dim past. Distance, presumably makes the Holocaust irrelevant. Americans also dismiss the subject as an "old world" problem; Europe's apocalyptic dance of death. By seeing the final

solution as an alien phenomenon, the Holocaust is safely relegated to the status of an academic historical curiosity. But as Eisenhower anticipated, America's relationship with the Holocaust could never be casual. The impulse to forget has jostled painfully against a reality impossible to ignore.

During the Nazi era, the American national myth of exceptionalism- a belief in Americans special destiny governed policies and passions. American's struggle with the depression and its unpleasant memory of having been manipulated into entering world war I promoted an isolationist mood. Few actually landed the ascendant national socialist movement in Germany (Pro-Nazi rallies in America, though frightening were marginal), but few actively opposed the Nazi's persecution of German Jews. After the Nazi boycott of Jewish stores in April 1993, for example, American reporters expressed outrage (briefly), but the Roosevelt administration remained indifferent.

In fairness, the signs of sustained anti-semitic violence in Nazi Germany were not easy for Americans to discern. The boycott was after all, a failure an indication that the situation might improve. Decrees in the spring of 1933 forbidding Jews to hold office seemed unimportant during the next two years of relative calm. Even the Nuremberg laws of 1935, prohibiting Germans and German Jews from mixing, seemed innocuous, interested in projecting a positive image to the rest of the world, especially during the Berlin Olympics in 1936, the Nazis were not eager to risk notoriety by enforcing racial policies.

Events in 1937-1938 drew the concern of the west for the first time. As the Nazis prepared for military dominance, they searched for ways to become self-sufficient independent, above all of Jewish participation in the Reich's economy by "Aryanizing" (Confiscating) Jewish businesses, they hoped to pressure Jews into leaving the Reich. Faced with the prospect of refugees seeking political asylum, the western nations, led by the United States, met in Evian, France, in July 1938. That conference presaged the world's indifference to the worsening situation in Nazi indifference to the worsening situation in Nazi occupied Europe. No nation was willing to open its doors. There was not even a resolution condemning Nazi anti-Semitic practices. The United States delegation announced only that it would continue admitting German and Austrian immigrants (among others), at the unimpressively rate of about 27,000 per year. (Between 1938 and 1941, the United States accepted a total of 124,000 immigrants) Sentiments at home were the decisive factors; these reflected the intense support for strict quotas; Americans feared competing with refugees for scare jobs, and many, prone to anti-semitism, were especially opposed to admitting Jews. Unintentionally, the Roosevelt administration sent a signal to the Nazis. The Nazis could feel free to find a radical "solution" to the Jewish problem.

The American entry into World War II in 1941 at last mobilized the nation against the Nazis. Although fighting to preserve democratic ideals, and determined to win the war, Americans showed little sympathy for the victims of genocide. Even when reports of the death camps, in 1942-1943, alerted American officials to the horror, no one with any authority budged. They wanted more evidence. At most, Roosevelt promised to rescue European Jews only through an allied victory. When, for example, it became possible to bomb the death camp Auschwitz - Birke -nau in 1943-1944, the Allies practically went out of their way to avoid doing so. Ways are found only to bomb a synthetic rubber works and SS barracks, a more 7 kilometers from Auschiwtz. With the exception of the war refugee board established early in 1944 to spirit Jews away from the Nazis, and the Oswego project (the relocation of hundreds of Jews to Oswego, New York), Jews were invisible victims of the Nazis. Only when the Allies liberated the death camps in 1945 did a few Americans finally begin to accept the enormity of the Nazi crimes.

Until the late 1970s, Americans were, for the most part, unwilling to grasp fully the facts of Nazi annihilation of close to six million European Jews. But there were several dramaticdevelopments that momentarily did disturb their apathy. First was the prosecution of Nazi criminals before the International military Tribunal (IMT) in Nuremberg in 1945-1946. In assembling the evidence, the prosecution offered explanations for the carnage that the world first learned about towards the end of the war. However, by focusing attention on Nazi criminals, the IMT maintained the veil that blinded the western world to the victims of the Nazi inferno.

During the 1950s, concern about the Nazi era receded to an all time low. Most survivors who managed to start a new life in the United States wanted to return to a 'normal' life. Their voices, which would eventually stir peoples' consciences, were momentarily still. But one event aroused renewed interest the publication of Anne Frank's diary. That moving testimony of one young girl's life in hiding in Amsterdam fascinated (and still fascinates) readers, especially young students who can easily understand Anne Frank's adolescent struggles. By expressing her ideals and hopes, however, it avoided discussing the suffering endured by so many Jews and other victims in favour of preserving a faith in mankind. Emblematic of the historical amnesia that characterized the 1950s, the diary overshadowed two seminal textual studies from this decade that defined the scope of the Nazi assault: Leon Poliakovs "Harvest of Hate: the Nazi Program for the destruction of the Jews of Europe" (French edition, 1951; English edition, 1954) and Gerald Reitlinger's" The Final solution. The attempt to exterminate the Jews of Europe, 1930-1945 (1953).

The year 1961 was the first of two major turning points in Americia's struggle to remember the Holocaust. Tellingly, Americans were still dependent on others for their information and insights. The lessons that Holocaust centers strive to teach deal, for the most part, with the consequences of prejudice and discrimination, the virtues of democracy, and how a commitment to democratic practices can help protect future generations from totalitarian templations, for example questions for discussion that end a unit in a curriculum typically ask students to consider what they might have done had they observed the persecution of Jews and what they believe are appropriate responses to the worldwide persecution of minorities today. The Holocaust era, therefore, provides ample case studies to sharpen a students moral and civic self awareness. This is an important educational objective, but it is not complete. It defines the historical study of the Holocaust era merely as a pretext for an interior discussion of issues facing Americans today. As a result, the programs and publications sponsored by most centers give less need than they should to the Holocaust era itself. Although, devoted to remembering the Holocaust, they are ironically engaged in more than little avoidance of the subject.

Ambiguity has characterized American reactions to the Holocaust in the past and today. This is true because Americans find themselves in the convenient position of not feeling forced to confront the Nazi past, the way Germans and Austrians are. Having defeated Nazism Americans, again and again, have been able to affirm their distance. By clinging to the national myths of the democratic experiment and historical exceptionalism, they have succeeded in keeping aloof. (The disclosures of French collaboration with the Nazis and French wartime anti-semitic initiatives have corroded the governing French-Gaullist myth of a nation that mobilized itself to resist the Nazi yoke).

But any past, and surely one so deeply resonant as the Nazi past, invades present day American life in spite of all the cultural defences erected against it. For American Jewery, the Holocaust has penetrated so completely that one observer, Jacob Neusner (stranger at Home, 1981) has branded the American Jewish community as a "fillowship of victimhood". He and others fear that an intense memory of the Holocaust is crowding out a creative awareness of Judaism as a religions and a heritage. Whether or not these critics are right, there is no doubt that American Jews have always been preoccupied with the Holocaust, during one week each year, the organized American - Jewish community observes the "days of remembrance", in Hebrew, "Yom hashoah".

Less explicit but at least as potent, is the legacy of the Holocaust era in the lives of other Americans. Is there not, for example, a new awareness that a nation can implement a policy of human extinction, and has not that awareness introduced an urgency to the basic impulse to survival? Has not this dreadful knowledge reinforced an anxiety about the future of humanity? Isn't it now accepted that innocent civilians can be mysteriously deemed an enemy and defined as a target for all our assault? This is the embryonic logic of modern Terrorism and contributes to the terrorism with which we still live. Given the proximity of violence in our time, is it any longer morally defensible to remain an onlooker? Doesn't such proximity confer new responsibilities on individuals as witnesses. After the Munich pact (the treaty authored in 1938 by British Prime Minister Neville Chamberlain to appease Nazi imperial ambitions) isn't neutrality the moral equivalent of complicity?

Americans like to see themselves as the main purveyors of ideals formed during the enlightenment, that intellectual revolution promoting faith in reason and progress. But no one the least bit familiar with the Holocaust can doubt that scientific progress can yield destructive as well as productive results. (In the shadow of the Holocaust, such technological hallmarks as the factory and its furnaces railroad trains, and medical discoveries forebode something deeply ominous). Religious and legal codes of ethics and the supremacy of the law have also been survived by Nazi practices and are susceptible to misuse. And because the Holocaust emerged from an advanced civilization, nurtured by the same ideals as those Americans cherish, no American can doubt that as civilization progresses so does it's destructive potential.

Traditional American myths and ideals have proven resilient in the face of the Holocaust. But do Americans cling to these beliefs from faith or from doubt ? If from faith, for the Holocaust has irrevocably transformed the postwar world.

C. The Holocaust Literature:

The Holocaust (Shoah), a disaster of Biblical proportions for European Jewery, forced Jewish-American literature to explore its impact on the world's largest, Diaspora community. In the process, novelists, both well and lesser known, and representing a variety of orientations to Judaism, have come to reflect on the meaning of covenantal existence and Jewish identity.

While the Holocaust is the fundamental orienting event for contemporary Jewish existence, raising in an intense manner questions about God, chosenness & and the nature of evil, Jewish, American novelists were slow to make it the orienting theme of their fiction. Separated by geography, history, and language from the agony of their fiction. Separated by geography, history, and language from the agony of their slaughtered European brethren, Jewish- American novelists, with few exceptions, continued for almost two decades after the Holocaust to display prewar modes of historical & theological innocence. They concerned themselves with issues such as assimilation and suburban Judaism or presented romanticized images of a vanished shtetl world. In the 1960s however, several events reminded Jews everywhere of their vulnerability. A plentitude of Holocaust novels and short stories emerged against this background, reflecting a growing awareness of the Holocaust's enormity for Jewish American life and thought Unike earlier Jewish-American fiction, this literature evaluated everything.

Though less successful at depicting the Holocaust experience, Jewish-American novelists successfully posed a plethora of related concerns important for both witnesses and non witnesses, European and American Jews alike. How, for example, can one imagine the unimaginable terrors of the death camps?

Theologically speaking does the covenant still exit? What kind of God permitted this tragedy to engulf His chosen people? What constitutes authentic Jewish living and literature and culture? These are only some of the ineluctable issues confronting Jewish-American novelists.

Problematics aside, Jewish American novelists have felt compelled to respond to the Holocaust. Among the first to do so, was Meyer Levin, whose 1959 novel 'Eva' tells the story of an escape from Auschwitz and the heroine's eventual arrival in Israel, where she marries and works in the legal profession. Subsequent Jewish-American writers can be understood as writers of indirection, lacking as they did; Lavin's historical experience as foreign correspondent during world war II and his Jewish and Zionist commitments. These writers utilized a variety of sources such as survivor testimony (Susan F. Schaeffer's 1974 novel 'Anya' is the clearest example) scholarly accounts (Saul Bellows' Mr. Sammler's Planet, 1970, and Leslie Epstein's 'King of the Jews', 1979) and the fundamental mythic ethos of biblical, rabbinic, and mystical Judaism in attempting to confront Auschwitz and its aftermath. Novels and short stories treating the complexities of post - Auschwitz Jewish existence constitute in fact a continuum of religious, secular, and symbolic responses.

I. Religious responses:

Religious responses to the Holocaust sharply distinguish between Jewish authenticity and American culture. They reflect what Ruth B. Wisse termed Act II of American Jewish writing. The Holocaust novels and short stories of Arthur A. Cohen, Hugh Nissenson, Cynthia Ozick, Chaim Potok, Isaac Bashevis Singer, and Elie Wiesel are uncompromising in their adherence to covenantal Judaism. Singer, a refugee from Poland, wrote several novels directly treating American Jewery, and the Holocaust ("Enemies, A love story", 1972, Shosha, 1978; and The Penitent, 1982"). Two of Wiesel's searing novels (The Accident, 1962, and the fifth son, 1985)" concern this theme. Taking their cue from the Europeans, the native born Jewish - American novelists confront the disaster by utilizing mystical and rabbinic motifs, classical teachings and messianic hopes as normatic guides for the Jewish imagination. Issues of faith and doubt are a palpable presence in the lives of their characters. God, the covenant, and the Jewish people are enmeshed in the search for post Auschwitz meaning.

The work of the late theologian and novelist Arthur A. Cohen is the model of religious response to the Holocaust. His Mammoth novel, "In the days of Simon Stern" (1973), combines magic, messianism, mysticism, and myth in outlining the continuing post-Holocaust struggle between good and evil very much in the Kabbalistic manner, Cohen underscores the tension between a diminished God and a mankind impatient to assume the role of diety in overturning evil. Unlike Ozick, however, Cohen was ambivalent about the state of Israel, viewing America as the resuscitator of post Holocaust Jewry.

II. Secular Responses:

Secular Jewish- American Holocaust literature reflects a preoccupation with the mystery of Jewish continuity. In individual works, Saul Bellow, Mark Helprin, Robert Kotlowitz, Bernard Malamud, Jay Meuge boren, and Susan F. Schaeffer distinguish between a Jewish authenticity rooted in Europe and a banalized American Judaism in which neither Jewish Kinship nor convenantal ethich play a role. In Mr. Sammler's planet 'Anya" and Cynthia Ozick's 'Rosa' (1983) the Holocaust not the covenant determines Jewish identity. For ex-survivors who were prewar assimilationist are, after the Holocaust, committed to Jewish kinship and a common Jewish destiny.

Saul Bellow's Mr. Sammler's planet potrays the prewar, Holocaust, and post Holocaust experiences of Arthur Sammler, a polish Anglophile who loses his wife and an eye during the Holocaust. He and his daughter survive and come to America. In New York city Sammler, the physically damaged survivor serves as a moral pivot for the assimilated, sexually promiscuous, and Jewishly indifferent relatives surrounding him. His message combines conveniently based ethics and a commitment to human obligation. Bellow/

Sammler posits this message as a counter to the culturally fashionable nihilism and apocalyptic mood of post - Auschwitz American life. Susan Scheaffer's 'Anya' follows the same biographical structure as Bellow's novel. Schaeffer tells the tale of Anya Savikin and her daughter. Anya is not religious in the traditional sense, although contending that she observes "in her own ways". Her survivor's message concerns the post Holocaust necessity of remaining Jewish.

This normative communal theme is also emphasized in an innovative way by Robert Kotlowitz in "The Boardwalk", his 1977 novel about Jewish America in 1939. Kotlowitz has written a post Holocaust critique of pre-Holocaust Jewish- American innocence. The novel's main character is a Hebrew- speaking veteran of world war I who had also lived in mandate Palestine. It is he alone who realizes the isolation of the Jews and the necessity of Jewish community. Kotlowitz also pinpoints the persistence of an ugly Jewish-American anti- Semitism. Three of Bernard Malamud's short stories, "The Loan" (1952), "The Lady Of The Lake" (1958) and "The German Refugee" (1963) despite their various settings (Europe and America) all portray the Holocaust as the point of entry into Jewish history for prewar assimilationsts and their recognition of the inescapability of Jewish identity and community.

III. Symbolic Responses:

Symbolic literary responses to the Holocaust are perhaps the most complex, novelists in this category either refrain from engaging the issue to Jewish specificity or highlight rifts within the Jewish community. Emphasis is placed on psychology more than theology. Questions of ethics, morality, and even those with theological overtones are asked outside the traditional covenantal framework. There is history, but little certainty of a Lord of history. There is a definable Jewish behaviour, but it is radically attenuated and eludes classical ritual formats. These writers focuson the complicated issue of post-Holocaust Jewish- Christian relations. The Holocaust works of Edward Lewis Wallant, Norma Rosen, and Philip Roth underscore these views.

Wallant's "The Pawnbroker (1961), though similar in structure both to "Anya" differs from them radically in universalizing the theme of human suffering and in potraying the survivor as Jewishly unreflective and indiffernet. Sol Nazerman, the Jewish survivor, is, for example, symbolically restored to spiritual wholeness only by the murder of his Christian assistant. Norma Rosen has written a novel with a far different type of universalism. Her "Touching Evil" (1969) boldly attempts to bring non-Jews into the universe of Jewish sensibility by describing the effects of the televised Eichmann trail on two Christian women. Rosen wisely understands that the Holocaust's evil is an enormous poison touching everyone. Philip Roth is the most complex of the writers in this group, His short stories and novels employ the Holocaust as a symbol of Jewish anthenticity against which he measures the behaviour and attitude of American Jews. Two short stories, "Defender of the Faith", and "Eli, the Fanatic" (both published in 1959), and two novels in particular, "The ghost writer" (1979) and "The counterlife" (1986) treat the issue of the Holocaust and Jewish identity. While admitting no easy summary, these works share a concern for post-Holocaust Jewish identity as it is forged either in the crucible of Jewish- Christian relations or within the Jewish community itself.

Epitomizing symbolic responses are the Holocaust novels of Leslide, Epstein, Bernard Malamud, and Hugh Nissenson.

Malamud's "The Fixer" (1966) and Nissenson's "My Own Ground" (1976) are symbolic prefigurations of the Holocaust. Malamud's novel is set in Europe and focuses on Czarist Russia's blood-libel trial of Mendel Beiliss, an antcedent war against the Jews, emphasizing Jewish vulnerability and the corruption of the modern state. Malamud, a master storyteller, is keenly aware of spiritual complexity, but his main character, Yaakov Bok, seems Jewishly indifferent. Betrayed by a fellow Jew, and rejecting God, Bok is befriended by Christians and seeks meaning in a symbolic community of the oppressed. Nissenson's novel takes place in the early teens of twentieth- century America. He, like Koilowitz, depicts and American jewery in process of dissolving its ties with tradition. Mystics, Marxists and Socialists all compete for the soul of America's Jews. A fortune telling mystic foresees the Holocaust; Unlike Malamud, however, Nissenson has written a novel whose main character, Jake Brody, while attracted by none of these options is Judicially knowledgeable although he neither practices nor believes in the tradition.

Epstin's "King of the Jews" (1979) is a historical fable concerning the plight of the Jews in the Lodz ghetto and of Mordechai Rumkowski, their mysterious and complex leader. Epstein's highly symbolic work employs gallows humor in fabulizing the historical predicament of the ghetto, thereby enabling his fictional Jews to gain a measure of transcendence over their oppressors that history itself cruelty denied them.

IV. Second - Generation literature:

A second generation Jewish - American literature of the Holocaust has began to appear. The second generation phenomenon had received some psychological attention in the late 1960s, but it was brought to public awareness with the appearance of Helen Epstein's journalistic account "Children of the Holocaust" (1979). Elie Wiesel's "The Fifth Son', dedicated to his son and to all children of survivors, legitizes this genre. The novel emphasizes the importance of remembrance for American non witnesses, those whom Wiesel describes as suffering from a history they never experienced but with which they are intimately acquainted through witnessing parents. In second generation fiction, children of Holocaust survivors struggle against evil, contend with the problematics of survivor parent -child relationship, and define their own quest for Jewish identity. Significant selected works in this genre include Thomas Friedmann's "Damaged Goods" (1984), Art Spiegelman's controversial "Maus" (1986), and Barbara Finkelstein's "Summer-Long-a coming" (1987). The issues of witnessing and authenticity remain problematic. Novels such as Robert "Greenfields Temple" (1982) and Frederick Busch's "Invisible Mending" (1984) use the genre without necessarily pentrating the issues.

There exists, moreover, a threefold red thread uniting the various expressions of Jewish - American Holocaust literature. Such literature takes seriously the search for meaning in history, recognizes that the Holocaust is a continuing trauma both for its survivors and their children, as well as for nonwitnesses, and it serves as a critique of human nature and contemporary civilization. There remains the difficulty of writing about the catastrophe of European Judaism when primary access to the event is through the imagination. But novelists can raise ultimate questions without being required to provide definitive responses. There is as well a recognition that America is increasingly the centre of Jewish renewal and creativity, and its literature is, therefore distinctively positioned to shed light on the continuing quest for authenticity in post Holocaust Jewish identity.

D. Orthodoxy:

Orthodox Judaism is the oldest of the three major branches of Judaism as established in the United States. It is committed to the maintenance of the Mosaic code as outlined in the "Torah" (Bible), the oral law (Talmud), and Jewish law as interpreted throughout the ages by the major rabbinic figures of their times and codified in the "Shulhan Arukh" (the code of Jewish Law)

The first congregations in the American colonies were established in accordance with orthodox ritual. Thus Shearith Israel, the oldest congregation in the United States, founded in New York in 1654, was orthodox. The ritual used by most of the colonial congregations was the western Europen version of the Sephardic rite. Besides congregations was the western European version of the Sephardic rite. Besides congregations, the early Jews also established "Mikvahs" (ritual baths), set up "Kosher¹ (ritually slaughtered) meat slaughtering facilities, and closed their stores on the Sabbath. Yet the New World with its professed policy of religious freedom posed many obstacles to traditional Jewish living. There were no rabbinic authorities, and the small numbers of Jews made intermarriage a problem. Indeed while the congregations were organized on traditional basis, only a small number of their members were in fact completely observant. The fact that America was not looked upon favourably by the European rabbinic authorities encouraged most observant European Jews not to come to America. (This attitude only changed in the mid twentieth century with the rise of Nazism in Germany) The United States did not have a fully ordained resident rabbi (Jewish priest) Until 1840, when Rabbi Abraham Rire (1802-1862) arrived from Germany Until 1881, few other orthodox rabbi followed suit. Yet until the 1840s Judaism in America was based on orthodox ritual, although there were few outstanding leaders or scholors. Gershom Mendes Seixas (1746-1816), the cantor and spiritual leader of New York's Shearith Israel Synagogue (Jewish Church) was perhaps the period's best known Orthodox leader, but he was largely self educated and hardly a scholar.

The arrival of thousand of central European Jews in the United States in the late 1830s and 1840s not only increased the Jewish population in the United States but also saw the start of the Reform movement, among the arrivals were influential Reform leaders such as Isaac M. Wise (1819-1900), David Einhorn (1809-1879), and Samud Adler (1809-1891). They and other Reform rabbis led a spirited and often bitter struggle to break the orthodox hold on Judaism and establish reform Judaism where they were largely successful is this struggle, they faced vehement orthodox opposition in their bid to reform Jewish ritual and synagogue practice. Isaac Lesser (1806-1868) stands out as the most prominent among the important orthodox Jewish leaders in mid nineteenth century America. From his pulpit in Philadelphia and his newspaper, "The Occident" (1843-1868), he led the battle against the Reform movement. Among his achievements was the establishment of the first American rabbinical college, Mainmonides College (1867) in Philadelphia. Other orthodox leaders were the previously mentioned Rice, who was the chief authority on Jewish law in the United states, Bernard Illowy (1812-1871) and Morris J. Raphael (1798-1868) of New York.

By the end of the civil war, Reform had come to dominate the Jewish religious scene in the United States and orthodoxy found itself on the defensive. Orthodoxy was limited to several dozen synagogues in the United States. One group of orthodox Jews were the old line Sephardic and German congregations who chose to remain loyal to their traditions. These "western" orthodox loyalists were led by Sabato Morais (1823-1897), Heniry Pereina Mendes (1852-1937), Bernard Drachman (1861-1945), and Henlry Schence Berger (1848-1916) of Baltimore. Another group of orthodox Jews were the recent immigrants from Eastern Europe centered in New York city. Their spiritual center was the Beth Medrash Hagadol Synagogue on New York's Lower East side. Its rabbi, Abraham J. Ash (1813-1888) was regarded as the group's senior spiritual leader. The western and eastern groups, although sharing a common allegiance to orthodoxy, differed on many points, such as the modernization of synagogue services, use of English and religious liturgical ritual. Thus there was little co-operation between them, and ultimately, the western orthodox group developed what orthodoxy later became conservative and modern orthodox Judaism. The eastern European orthodox groups evolved into a more fundamentalist orthodoxy.

The mass immigration of hundreds of thousands of Jews to the United States from Czarist Russia starting in 1881 reinforced orthodoxy within 10 years, hundreds of new orthodox synagogues and prayer houses were established. What had been perceived as a dying orthodoxy suddenly underwent a revival. Besides synagogues, traditional orthodox institutions evolved, such as Kosher butcher stores, ritualariums (Mikvah), religious schools and the like.

However, leadership and organization was lacking because there were no prestigious scholars among the new comers and hardly any English speaking orthodox rabbis. Thus, each group of orthodox Jews developed its own way of solving these problems.

The "western" orthodox group, with the financial support and moral ecouragement of prominent reform lay leaders such as Louis Marshall (1856-1929) and Jacob Schiff (1847-1920) established the Jewish Theological Seminary (1886) as a rabbinical seminary to train English speaking secularly educated rabbis for all segments of American orthodoxy. Indeed, until its reorganization in 1902, the Seminary was an orthodox school, whose faculty consisted of men like Morais, Mendes and Druchman. Yet the Eastern European orthodox population and rabbinate looked down on the seminary because of its inferior level of Talmudic study.

The western group also established the Union of Orthodox Jewish congregations of America in 1889 as a means of solving the leadership and organizational problem of American orthodoxy. This organization, however failed to attract any significant following among the eastern European Jews until well into the twentieth century.

The Eastern European Jews sought to solve the problem of rabbinic leadership by setting up a Chief Rabbinate for New York. In 1888, they installed a well-known Lithuanian rabbi, R. Jacob Joseph (d.1902), as Chief Rabbi of New York. Although this experiment failed the fact that a man of Rabbi Joseph's stature would come to America encouraged other eastern European rabbis to immigrate to the United States. By the twentieth century, there were a number of competent rabbinical authorities residing in the north east. Following Rabbi Joseph's death in 1902, these recognized eastern European rabbis formed an organization called Agudath Ha- Rabbonim the Union of orthodox Rabbis of the United States.

This group sought to set standards for the rabbinate and exert leadership on behalf of Orthodox Jewry in the United state, and it remained the most significant orthodox tribune until the 1950s. Among its leaders were Rabbis Eliezer Sillver (1882-1968), Israel Rosenberg (1875-1956), Mosses S. Margolies (1851-1936), Bernard Leventhal (1865-1952), and Geffen Tobias (1870-1970) The problem of producing future generations of native rabbis for the United States did not generally concern the eastern European orthodox leaders as they could always import European rabbis.

This attitude greatly hurt orthodoxy in its efforts to pass its traditions on the second generation, American born

Jewish successors. Yet, in 1897, a small traditional Yeshiva or Talmudic academy, was started in New York on the lower east. side. It was not designed as a rabbinical college but rather as a place of study for young European rabbinical scholars who had come to America, even so, a number of these refugee scholars did eventually become rabbinical and educational leaders in the United States. This small school named for the late Chief Rabbi of Kovna, Isaac Elhanan Spektor (1817-1896), eventually grew or become Yeshiva college and later Yeshiva University under the leadership of Bernard Revel (1885-1940).

By the beginning of world war I, a full-scale orthodox Jewish life existed in most Jewish communities in the United States with 500 or more Jews. These communities had synagogues, rabbis, teachers, ritual slaughters and schools among other institutions. The heart of orthodox Jewish life was located in major cities such as New York, Philadelphia, Chicago, and Baltimore. But orthodoxy could not hold the second generation American Jew. The powerful forces of assimilation, secularization, socialism upward mobility and Americanization in general made orthodoxy look "old world", primitive, foreign, and associated with the poverty of the first generation immigrants. Orthodoxy had failed to produce an English - speaking rabbinate and had not set up any meaningful effective school system to teach its beliefs to the younger generation. Yet, it must be added that a small number of American - born or educated youth did remain orthodox and attempted to build an American version of orthodoxy.

With the end of world war I, orthodoxy faced new challenges. As mass emigration, from Eastern Europe to the United states declined orthodoxy found dependent on attaining the loyalties of second generation American Jews. As a religious group, Orthodoxy was challenged by conservative Judaism, an outgrowth of the previously orthodox Jewish Theological Seminary. Conservative Judaism its loyalty to tradition, yet was in favor of significant change in ritual, liturgy, and practice; In its battle with orthodoxy, it held upper hand until well into the 1960s.

However, the small group of second generation orthodox followers took step to build a new and more attactive orthodoxy, which was organized in New York city.

The Rabbi Isaac Elhanan Rabbinical School was reorganized as a high school (1916) and a college - Yeshiva- (1925) and a formal rabbinic program was established in the 1920s to produce American trained, English - speaking, orthodox rabbis. Under the leadership of Bernard Revel, Yeshiva College became the undisputed center of Talmudic scholarship and orthodox Judaism in the United States until well into the 1970s. By the late 1920s, a small cadre of English-speaking orthodox rabbis were in place. The Hebrew Theological college, an institution similar to Yeshiva college, was founded in Chicago in 1922 with Rabbi Saul Silber (1881-1946) as its president. Several smaller rabbinical schools also existed in Brooklyn and the lower east side at this time. Graduates of these schools as well as other English speaking orthodox rabbis, founded the rabbinical council of America in 1935. Among the prominent members of the Rabbinical council were rabbis Joseph H. Lookstein (1902-1979) rabbi of New York's fashionable Kehillah Jeshurun Synagogue and founder of the -Ramaz Day School (1936). Herbert S. Goldstein (1890-1970) of the west side

Institutional Synagogue, Leo Jung (1892-1987) of New
York's Jewish center, Samuel Rosenblatt of Baltimore (b.
1902), and David de Sola Pool (1885-1970) of New Yorks'
Shearith Isarael Synagogue.

Together with the union of orthodox Jewish
Congregations and the newly created National council of
Young Israel Synagogues (1912), a loose alliance of English -
speaking orthodox congregation aimed at second and third
generation Americans, was created and thus, the institutional
framework for what was to be called modern orthodoxy was
put in place. With the appointment in 1939 of Rabbi Joseph
B. Soloveintchik (b.1903) as head of the Talmud faculty of
Yeshiva college, modern orthodoxy gained a respected and
influential leader who was to dominate modern orhtodoxy
well into the present.

As modern orthodoxy emerged, there was also the
corresponding development of a new American - style
traditional orthodoxy. This movement was centered in the
Williamsburg section of Brooklyn, around the Mesifta
Torah V'daath (f-1917), directed by Rabbi Shraga Feivel
Mendelowitz (1886-1948). Under Mendelowitz's leadership
this school had grown from a small elementary school to
include a rabbinical program with prominent scholars on the
faculty. What separated Torah V'daath from Yeshiva college
was a more restrained attitude toward secular ducation, the
western culture, as well as a strider interpretation of Jewish
law. Yet at that point (the 1930s) all were part of the same
orthodox grouping.

During this time, one could also detect the beginnings
of a home grown American Hasidic Movement. Although
tens of thousands of masidim (mostly lubavitch) had arrived

in the United States prior to the world was I, few if any were able to pass their traditions on to a second generation. Following a year long visit to the United State in 1929, the sixth lubavitcher Rebber; Rabbi Joseph I. Schnerroshn (1880-1950), revived interest in Hasidism among American orhtodox youth. Several small lubavitch groups were established in New York, and several dozen young Men travelled to Poland to study under Schenner Shon's tutelage.

The 1930's also saw the establishment of a number of orthodox Jewish high schools, which eventually grew into rabbinical colleges. Among the better known were Yeshivah chaim Berlin in Brooklyn (1939), under the leadership of a charismatic scholar from Europe, Rabbi Isaac Hunter (1907-1980), Yeshivah Tifferth Jerusalam (1937), in Manhattan under the leadership of Rabbi Moses Feinstein (1895-1986), who was eventually to become the leading authority on Jewish law in the United States; and the Ner Israel Yeshiva in Baltimore (1933), under the leadership of Rabbi Jocob I. Ruderman (1901-1987). Yet, until world war II, orthodoxy in the United States was still dominated by the old line Yiddish -speaking rabbi, synagogue, and laymen. The voice of orthodoxy was still predominantly the voice of the poor, the refugee, and the uneducated.

With the rise of Nazism in Germany and later in Austria, a new stream of Jewish immigrants arrived in the United States. Among them were a small group of highly dedicated and educated orthodox Jews. A group of orthodox Jews from Germany reorganized themselves in the Washington heights section of New York under the leadership of Rabbi Joseph Brever (1892-1980) This group, known as Khal Adas Jeshurun, built a full scale orthodox community with a synagogue, school system, and a Kashruth network. This group played an important role in proving that orthodoxy could be transplanted to the United States, with its strict standards intact.

Austrian refugees included a large number of orthodox Jews who belonged to the strict separatist tradition of Hungarian Orthodox Jewry. They set up a number of schools and synagogues in New York under the leadership of scholars like Rabbi Samuel Ehrenfled (d.1970) of Matltesdorf, Austria and Rabbi Levi Y. Grunewald (d. 1980) of Deutsh Kreutz, Austria. Grunewald was responsible for raising the standards of Kosher milk and meat in the United States and laid the groundwork for the post world war II Hasidic influx to New York.

The onset of world war II brought tens of thousands of orthodox Jews to the United States in the period between 1939 and 1951. Among these were prominent rabbis, Yeshiva deans, Hasidic leaders and their follower, and lay orthodox Jews. As a rule, the new immigrants were better educated in Judaism than their American counterparts and more concerned about Jewish education for their children.

Prominent among the Yeshiva deans to arrive was Rabbi Aaron Kotler (1892-1962) of Kletzk, Poland, Kotler a universally recognized Talmudist, immediately reogranized his Yeshiva in Lakewood, New Jersey (1941). Upon his death his school had 250 advanced students, and in 1988 it numbered over 1000 students Kotler inculcated American orthodox Jews with a love for Torah study and preached that the highest form of Jewish life was the study of Torah. Thus, together with his European colleagues he set up various rabbinical schools and 'Kolels' (advanced institutes for rabbinic studies) across the United States. By the 1960s, these schools, and their deans, had become a major force in American orthodox life. This group of American orhtodoxy, known as Yeshiva world, was organized around the Agudath Israel of America, whose dominating figure was Rabbi Musha Sherer. The Agudah was governed by a council of Torah Sages consisting primarily of Yeshiva deans. Since 1945, it's membership has included Rabbi Aaron Kotler, Moses Feinstein, Shneur Kotler (d. 1982) Jacob Kaminetsky (1891-1986), Israel Spiro (1897-1989), Isaac Hutner, and Jacob Ruderman. The organ of the Agudath was the Jewish observer.

The Modern orthodox camp, the Yeshiva world, and Rabbi Mendelowitz joined forces to organize the Torah U' Mesorah Movement (f. 1944) the National council of Jewish Day Schools, which sought to establish orthodox day schools across the United States. By the 1960s the movement came under the domination of the 'Yeshiva World. Schools were established in cities with 5000 or more Jews, and a number of high schools and seminaries were also established.

A large number of Hasidic Jews, primarily from Hungary, arrived after world war II. The two most prominent Hasidic rabbis were the Satmar Rabbe, Rabbi Joel Teitelbaum (1886-1979), and the Lubavitcher Rebbe, Rabbi Joseph I. Schneerson (1880-1950) from Russia via Poland Teitel baum and other rebbes like him, chiefly from Hungary and Romania, sought to reestablish their communities here exactly as they were in Europe. They sought to preserve the dress, Yiddish language, and customs of Eastern Europe. As such, they were very successful. They established schools, synagogues, and a Koshar food industry. It has been estimated (1988) that there are over 100,000 Hasidim in the United States, centered primarily in metre politan New York, and their numbers are growing. Other prominent Hasidic leaders who built communities similar to Teitel baum's were the Bobover Rebbe, Rabbi Solomon Halberstan (b. 1908) the Poper Rav, Rabbi Joseph Grunwald (d. 1984) the Kluzenberger Rebbe, Rabbi Y. Y. Halberstam (b. 1904), and the Skverer Rebbe, Rabbi Jacob Twersky (d. 1968).

Orthodox Judaism has clearly established itself in America. It has a viable infrastructure of schools, synagogues, and other religions institutions. It is rapidly shedding its refuge image and has become very acculturized. Its committed and learned laity, as well as its educated and effective rabbinical leadership, promises that orthodoxy will continue to be a vital force in the American Jewish community as we approach the twenty first century.

E. Anti Semitism:

A significant percentage of Americans, perhaps as many as 20 to 25 percent still harbor anti-semitic stereotypes. Gary Tobin in his book "Jewish Perceptions of Anti Semitism"(1988) has demonstrated that Jews on the whole feel that anti-semitism is still a problem. They point to the greater visibility of neo-Nazi political tendencies in western Eurpoe, Canada, and the United States and the growth of Holocaust revisionism. In 1985, for example, Canada witnessed the much publicized trails of Ernst Zundel in Ontario and Jim Kelgstra in Alberta, both dealing with the denial of the Holocaust. They are disturbed when organizations such as the white Aryan Resistance, the Aryan Nations, the order, and the Revitalized Ku Klux Klan promulgate antisemitic and racist rhetoric and literature and indicate their intention to do acts of violence against blacks and Jews. They are concerned when bigoted groups of youth known as "Skinheads" are growing across the country, possibly numbering as many as 3500 in 35 cities, and are being supported by older racist groups.

These groups have been blamed for crimes ranging from intimidation and arson to murder. Jews are made anxious by the increased violence directed against them, including such heinous crimes as the bombing of synagogues, the desecration of cemeteries, and the assassination by Aryan extremists of Denver radio personality Alan Berg in 1984. Finally, they are made uneasy by the blurring of the distinctions between genuine criticism of specific Israeli policies and vitriolic anti-Zionist diatribes riticism that go well beyond legitimate political criticism or discourse and that use Israel as a surrogate for traditional anti - Semitic beliefs and attitudes, the rise of a fundamental christainity that claims that God does not hear the prayers of Jews; the apparent increase of black anti-Semitism, and the anti Semitic slurs of a candidate for the Unitd States presidency.

To be sure, a difference exists between Europe and America, but has America been different enough? "This question is central enough ever since a once civilized countery exploded in this century in an unprecedented orgy of anti-semitism and genocide. It is a question that permits no easy answers.

Historians of American Jewry have tended to view anti-Semitism as an exception, a quirk of fate, an abnormal situation caused by temporary social and economic factors. Notwithstanding the tendency of many to see anti-Semitism behind every furtive glance and frustarated desire, clearly not every negative statement or sentiment regarding Jews is anti -Semitic. To some extent, Jewish immigrants to America experienced hostility simply for being impoverished an accultured foreigners. American pride in this country as a haven for the oppressed and the liberal traditions of tolerance individuality and equal opportunity and equal opportunity helped create the ambivalent attitudes that Americans have had concerning Jews, often combining feelings of hostility with feelings of friendship and acceptance. Moreover mitigating circumstances contributed toward tolerance within the historical tradition of American Christianity. John Higham, the historian, has argued, for example, that certain strain of sentiment among American Protestants admired Jews and Judaism. Puritan orthodoxy held that the Jews were Gods chosen people, miraculously saved and sustained as proof of God's greatness a view that lent itself to sympathy and positive identification with the Jews.

Because of these factors, scholars of the American experience did not really look at the issue of anti-semitism until after the Holocaust. Prominent social scientists and psychologist, in the wake of that tragedy, attempted to analyze and understand the social, economic, religious, cultural and psychological factors that predisposes some individuals and societies to reactions of extreme hostility and hatred directed toward racial and religious groups. The writing of Theodor Adorno, Bruno Bettelheim, Morris Janowitz, Seymour Martin Lipset, Alan Davies, Gordon All port, Charles Stember, Rodney Stark, and Harold Quinley are indicative of the vast social science research that has been done in this area.

In particular, Glock and Stark, in "Christain Beliefs and Anti Semitism" (1966), propounded a correlation between professing anti-semitic beliefs and levels of Christian affiliation. Gary Marx's "Protest and Prejudice" (1969) found blacks no more anti-Semitic than whites, to the extent that black anti-semitism exists, it results largely from unfavourable social and economic contact between Jew and black.

"The Tenacity of Prejudice" (1969), a survey analysis by Selznick and Steinberg, isolates the independent variables that contribute to anti-semitism. The researchers developed an "Index of Anti-Semitic Belief", which they submitted to 2000 respondents. Analyzing the results, they found that education, more than age, generation, geographical location, culture and religious beliefs, was the most important independent variable in determing to extent of anti-semitic bias. They went on to predict the gradual disppearance of anti-Semitism with the spread of education.

"Anti-Semitism in the United States. A study of Prejudice in the 1980s" (1982) by Gregory Martire and Ruth dark, is very much in the same tradition. Also using survey analysis, the authors attempt to provide "the first comprehensive trend study of anti-Semitism in the United States, and to examine the factors that are associated with American anti-Semitism in the 1908s. "Drawing on the Selznick and Steinberg study, pule a 1977 study on attitudes toward Israel by Yankelovich, Skelly, and white, Inc., Martire and Clark conducted 50 in -depth interviews with Jews and non-Jews from across the nation and complied a quantitative survey based on

1215 personal interviews representing all adult groups in the contiguous United States.

The authors conclude that, although a minority, "Individuals holding anti-Semitic beliefs clearly represent a significant social problem in the United States. "One in four whites (23 percent) can be characterized as prejudiced. Though anti-Semitic beliefs continue to present a serious problem, the authors found a decline since 1964 in the prevalence of many traditional anti-Semitic stereotypes, such as negative images relating to shrewdness, dishonesty, assertivenss or willingness to use shady business practices. The decline resulted not from changes in the attitudes of individuals but rather from generational change the coming of age of those who were children in the mid-1960s, who as young people tended to be relatively, unprejudiced and who showed an increased tolerance of diversity.

Martine and Clark did not find any particular correlation between political conservation, energy crisis concerns, dual loyalty fears, or religious fundamentalism and anti-Semitism, Instead, their study indicates that anti-Semitism is associated most strongly with three demographic characteristics: age, education and race. "The level of anti-Semitism is higher among adults who are older, less educated, or black", thus pointing to the generational variables as the most important determinant. This finding has a number of significant implications for the authors". It suggest that an individual's attitude toward Jews is probably relatively enduring. It also suggests that the decline in anti-Semitism should continue as the better educated and more tolerant young adults continue through the life cycle".

The only exception to this hopeful prognosis is the black community. The authors found that race is the other demographic factor most closely associated with anti-Semitism. About 23 percent of whites can be characterized as prejudiced compared to 37 percent of blacks. Black anti-Semitism appears to stem primarily from the tensions caused by the middleman minority, or retailer consumer, relationship that characterizes the economic, interactions of the two groups. Notwithstanding that these studies have made an important contribution to the growing body of social science literature on the subject of anti-Semitism, some weaknesses in the approach need highlighting, Since such studies lack a historical orientation and because, as Lucy Dawidowicz pointed out in her book "The Jewish Presence" (1977) of "its single focus on opinion", the survey analysis method is "not properly geared to study the etiology of anti-Semitism. Useful for periodic pulse taking, it nevertheless serves ultimately to limit our understanding of anti-Semitism, which is a phenomenon marked by a high "degree of multiformity and contradictoriness". Furthermore, these works of social research do not explain the earlier and specifically American manifestations of anti-Semitism.

Beginning in the late 1960s, American scholars apparentlybecame more sensitive to the issue of American anti-Semitism and the role of ideology. Critical of the grading over process of consensus historiography, they initiated a revisionist critique of the problem. Several factors account for the problem. Several factors account for this development. American historians of the time engaged generally in a critical rethinking of assumptions long taken for granted concerning the political, economic, and social realities of our past. American Jewish scholars, just beginning to come into their own in academia, were drawn towardaspects of the American Jewish experience previously unexamined. The pluralistic attitudes characteristic of the 1960s'culture brought Jews and Jewish scholars out of the closet so to speak, and made it easier for them to discuss publicly issues of Jewish concern. The growing interest in the Holocaust, spurred on by the 1961-1962 Eichmann trial, the 1967 Arab-Israeli war and predications of second Holocaust, and the emergence of Elie wilser as folk hero and witness to atrocity generated interest in the problem of anti-Semitism.

In addition, Israel's creation in 1948 had posed theological problems for many Christians. These people believed that Judaism ceased as a creative and legitimate force with the rise of Christianity and that the destruction of the Temple had marked the death of Judaism and the Jewish people as viable, living entities. The perception that Jews were a "fossilized relic of Syriac society" as British historian Arnold Tonybee put it, apparently made it difficult for many Christians to support the modern state created by this "anachronistic" people. Yet these negative factors, one can surmise, facilitated a positive response in some areas and a renewed interest in Jewish Christian relations in America and the desire to look closely and critically at the problem of American anti-Semitism.

Nineteenth- century American society probably was unaware of the European historical background that had built anti Semitism into its societal structure. Except for a few knowledgeable individuals, America hardly know of the medieval ecclesiastical statutes limiting the types of economic activity available to Jews. Consequently, while the origins of the structurally created anti-Semitism in European and American society had been forgotten, the symbolic expressions of these origins remained embedded in the literature and sensibilities of western society in the form of pejorative sterotypes.

What is the relationship of there images to the tendency todiscriminate against Jews? Do all negative images lead inevitably to discrimination? Are some more dangerous than others? What elements in society benefit from discrimination? What impact have these negative images had on Jewish self-perception and self -esteem? Has their existence fostered the rush towards assimilation?

Among the relatively few books and articles that examine American anti-Semitism from a historical perspective, one finds only tentative answers to these questions. The best-known works-the studies by Oscar Handlin, John Higham, Arnold Rose, Leonard Dinnerstein (The Leo Frank case) 'Corey MC Williams, and Richard Hofstadter' - argue that ant- 'Semitism it the consequence of objective socieconomic factors and tensions operative in society that affect marginal groups. Sander Diamond (1974) and Lea Ribuffo (1980) have extended this analysis of social conflict to include those individuals who have created or joined radical right and Christian right organizations.

The relationship between Christian orthodoxy and anti-Semitism is due almost entirely to three demographic factors education, race and age. After controlling for education, race and age, we find that the partial correlation between religiousness and anti-Semitism virtually disappears, indicating that the apparent relationship is actually due to the fact that individuals who are traditional in their religious outlook are more likely to be older, less educated and black- all factors that are associated with higher levels of anti-Semitic belief.

Anti-Semitic ideology and anti-Semitic attitudes are insufficientin themselves to explain America's anti-Jewish tendencies. Most contemporary analyses of American anti-Semitism show, disturbingly, that in the late-nineteenth and early twentieth centuries, anti-Semitism was separated from analysis of capitalist development, thereby locating the American- Jewish problem in a structural vacuum independent from other economic or social tendencies.

Yet the fact remains that anti-Semitism erupted even in reformist and libertarian sectors of American society. The democratic impulse was not and may not be always esolute enough to overcome the psychological and social momentum of anti-Semitic stereotyping. True, America never visited mass physical oppression upon its Jews. But there are more subtle types of oppression-economic, social and cultural that are also damaging and painful.

Discrimination at summer resorts, private schools, and clubs increased during the years before world war I The century club in New York rejected the distinguished scientist Jacques Loeb because he was a Jew, Most Masonic lodges excluded Jews. Some of the most prestigious preparatory schools, such as Exeter; Hotchkiss, and Andover, had small Jewish quotas. After 1900, few Jews were elected to the Princenton clubs or to the fraternities at Yale, Columbia, and Harvard. The literary and gymnastic societies at Columbia kept Jews out entirely. As a result, Jewish students gradually formed their own fraternities, the first appearing at Columbia in 1898. The anti-Semitic feelings also infected college facilities. It was common knowledge that few Jews could gain entry or advancement in American academic circles.

Social discrimination reached a climax in the quota systems adopted by college and medical schools in the years after world War I. Many colleges set limits on Jewish enrollment. Some established alumni committees to screen applicants. Others under the pretext of seeking regional balance, gave preference to students outside the East, thereby limiting the number of Jews, who were heavily concentrated there. The most common method of exclusion came with the introduction of character and psychological examinations.

Before the 1920s, scholastic performance was the most important criteria used in admissions policies. Now admission committees devised tests to rank students on such characteristics as "public spirit", "fair play", "interest in fellows", and "leadership", traits not usually associated with Jews in the popular mind. Here, we see that negative imagery can have social consequences.

According to the prevailing opinion, "public spirit" and "interest in fellows" were Christian virtues, Jews were excessively clannish and cared only for their group, "Leadership", again was seen as a protestant virtue; Jews exhibiting it would be regarded as aggressive and pushy. By 1919, New York University instituted stringent restrictions and introduced psychological testing. Chancellor elmor Brown justified this policy, citing the "separateness" of the Jewish student body. Columbia University cut the number of Jews in the incoming classes from 40 to 20 percent. At Harvard, where elite Protestant students and faculty reared the University's becoming a "new Jerusalem", President A. Lawrence Lowell in 1922 recommended a quota system, openly adopting what other institutions were doing covertly. "There is a rapidly growing anti-Semitic feeling in this country", he wrote in June of that year "Caused by a strong race feeling on the part of the Jews. "Smaller colleges, perhaps more rigid than some large, urban ones, used more subjective criteria, such as requiring a. photograph of the candidate and enforcing a geographic distribution. This was even a greater problem in Medical schools, where formidable barriers spread throughout the country, severly limiting Jewish enrollments and causing undue hardship. So, what began quite explicitly at Columbia, New York University and Harvard, namely the adoption of a Jewish quota, reflected what was going on behind the scenes, between 1920 and the Mid-1940s, at most eastern private liberal arts colleges and elite universities, in the major state universities in the south and mid west and nationally in many medical, dental and law schools.

As Marcia Graham Synnott has argued, the reasons for these limitations were "to perpetuate the economic and social position of middle and upper-middle-class, white, native-born Protestants". This policy also had social and economic implications since few manufacturing companies corporate law firms, private hospitals or such government bureaucracies as the State Department welcomed Jews".

In 1920s also saw the proliferation of the "restrictive covenants" in housing where owners pledged not to sell their homes and property to Jews and other undersirable groups. Economic discrimination also grew. In banking, insurance, and public utilities firm, Jews could not find positions. Employment agencies also found that Jews were unacceptable to most employers. The Alliance employment Bureau in New York city, for example, wrote to Cyrus Sulzberger, president of the United Hebrew Charities, in 1928. "We are finding great difficulty in placing our Jewish boys and girls, and increasing number of employers absolutely refusing to take them."The Katharine Gibbs School for secretarial training informed a Jewish applicant in 1928 that it's policy was "not to accept students of Jewish nationality" Insurance companies, such as Connecticut Mutual Life Insurance Co, the Shawnee Fire Insurance Co, and the New Jersey Fire Insurance Co, urged their agents not to insure Jewish clients because they are "an extaordinary hazardous class".

The most significant ideological attack against Jews also occurred during the 1920s and 1930s. It focused not on religious issues or Jewish social climbing but on race and political subversion. A resurgent Ku Klux Klan activated the polluters. More significantly, the country witnessed the resurrection, of the international stereotype of the Jew as half banker and half Bolshevik; conspiring to seize control of the nation. This belief, having been foreshadowed during the civil war, emerged in the 1980s during the Populist ferment and crystallized in the early 1920s around auto Magnate Henry Ford. In May 1922, Ford's newspaper, the Dearborn "Independent, launched an anti-Semite propoganda campaign without precedent in American history. It lasted for about seven years. In time the newspaper "exposed" Jewish control of everything from the League of Nations to American politics, from baseball and jazz to agriculture and movies. If any pattern of ideas activated discriminations, it was the conspiratorial ferment to which the populists, Henry Ford, and the KKK contributed.

With the approach of world war II, these issues were further clouded by events in Europe. As Hitler proved to be virulently anti-Semitic, American Jews began to argue for intervention in the affairs of Europe, a stand resented by isolationists committed to keeping America out of the impending conflagration. On September 11, 1941, American aviation head Charles Lindbergh warned that the Jews and President Roosevelt were conspiring to bring the nation into a war against Germany and that such a war would prove catastrophic for America.

The situation became more acute when European Jews began to seek refuge in this country. The growing isolationism and xenophobia of the 1930s, as well as public opinion polls of the period, have shown how stereotyping reinforced insensitivity and misunderstanding and contributed to governmental inerta in the face of an unprecedented human tragedy. The critical decade of the 1930s witnessed the rise of Nazism in Europe as well as a high degree of acceptance and approval of anti-Semitism in America. Although sympathetic to the plight of the refuges, many Americans remained unalterably opposed to admitting them.

When we add up all the individual cases of American anti-Semitism before world war II, they may not seem very significant. But when viewed differently, the callous lack of concern for Nazi refugees and refusal to admit them that led to certain death for countless thousands, the reality becomes painfully disturbing.

However, matters began to improve dramatically after 1945. Whether as a result of guilt feelings and sympathy for Jews because of the Holocaust, or the greater effectiveness of American Jewish organizations committed to fighting anti-Semitism, or the diminished appeal of ideologies of all sorts in postwar America, the fact is that the intensity and effect of anti-Semitism in the United States declined significantly in the late 1940s and 1950s. Universities and colleges began to loosen their quota restrictions. Medical, dental and law schools showed dramatic increases in the numbers of Jewish students Public opinion polls in the early 1950s began reflecting the more positive attitudes that non-Jews had concerning Jews. Major public opinion surveys published in 1964, 1966, 1981 and 1982 indicated that the trend was continuing.

Institutional discrimination against Jews in housing and employment was sharply reduced. Jews began to enjoy greater political success. Jews were elected to the congress, the Senate, and other high political offices, in numbers far disproportionate to the size of the Jewish population. In the 101st congress sworn in on January 3, 1989, there were 31 Jewish Members of the House of representatives and 8 Jewish Senators, one of whom is believed to be the first orthodox Jews elected to the chamber. By the 1980s, some would feel that anti-Semitism in the United states once a serious problem, was a thing of the past.

While there is no question that Americans today are much more accepting the Jews and far less intolerant than they were in the pre-world war II period, there still are some significant areas of concern. There is one notable exception to the apparent decline of anti-Semitic attitudes and it appears in the black community with which Jews have been historically linked in their collective struggles for civil rights and equal opportunities. Recent public opinion surveys reveal that on almost every indicator blacks, particularly young blacks, hold more negative views of Jews than whites. This is troubling for two reasons. First, contrary to what is happening among whites, black anti-Semitism is inversely related to age and education (the strongest anti Semitism is expressed by the most educated and by younger blacks). Second, although anti-Semitism is not now generally politically acceptable in America, the one exception to this is in the black community. The more politically conscious and active blacks appear to be more negative than the majority of blacks. When such very public personalities as Jesse Jackson used terms like "hymies" to refer to Jews during his 1984 campaign for the Democratic presidential nomination and when he, and other black leaders, did not repudiate Louis Farrakhan who introduced anti-Semitic rhetoric into national politics, and gave a muted response to congressman Gus Savages remarks, about Jews, then there is cause for concern. What this indicates is that the historic alliance between Jews and blacks, forged during the long civil rights struggle seems to be drawing to a close. The sources for these tensions go back several decades. As early as the 1960s, many black activities began to feel that Jews in the civil rights. Movement were patronizing in their attitudes and were reluctant to give up leadership roles to blacks. Meanwhile there were developments in American society that brought new conflicts between blacks and Jews. The population of blacks in America's Northeast cities,where Jews lived in disproportionate numbers, continued to increase, and this caused social friction between adjacent black and Jewish communities. Jews, like other whites, tended now to link the problem of crime to the"problem" of the blacks. Resentment and fear intensified and they surfaced with acute force during such controversies as the New York city teacher's strike of 1968. That strike developed over the issue of school decentralization, the catalyst was a decision made by the Ocean Hill- Brownsville board in April 1968 to dismiss 19 teachers considered in opposition to the experimental project in decentralization. Almost all were Jews.

When Superintendent of Schools Bernard Donovan called for the reinstatement of the teachers, local parents, most of whom were blacks, prevented the teachers from entering the schools. In September, approximately 95 percent of the teachers went on strike. The lines were now drawn between a white, largely Jewish school system and the United Federation of Teachers facing a largely black student and parent body. This situation unleashed a plethora of racist and anti-Semitic expressions that appeared in print and on the radio, like the anti-Semitic poem, written by a 15-year old schoolgirl read on WBAI - FM on December 26, 1968.

"Hey, Jew Boy, with that Yarmulka on your head". Remarks like these and the tensions they unleashed led many Jews to fear that black anti-semitism was a serious concern. Furthermore recalling a history of quota systems and anti-Semitic hiring practices in the United States, many fell that the merit system was the Jew's one protection and this was threatened by differences between the two communities on social issues such as decentralization, affirmative action quotas, busing, political rights, and economic competition. Differences over Israel exacerbated the problem. Many blacks identify with liberation struggles around the globe and have aligned themselves with the Arab and PLO struggles against Israel. This is legitimate when it is based on reasoned, careful analyses of the situation. Unfortunately, it often blends into an anti-zionism verging on anti-Semitism when Israel is unfairly described as a kind of conspiratorial state with demonic qualities characterized by its alleged arrogance and it's colonialist, imperialist, and racist tendencies.

In the overall community, new stereotypes have emerged and younger non-Jews are more likely than older non-Jews to hold them. Education and generation appears not to have brought the hoped for end to anti-Semitism. Stereotypic Jewish American Princess Jokes, for example, and "JAP-bating" generally may not always be intended as anti-Semitism but may reveal latent prejudice. Ultimately, it is the relationship between attitude and behaviour that is important here and it may not be much consolation that only 20 to 25 percent of Americans have anti-Semitic attitudes in light of the apparent increase of anti-Semitic incidents in recent years. Audits of anti-Semitic incidents produced by the Anti-Defamation League since 1979 show an average of over 600 reported occurrences a year. The number has grown from about 400 in 1980 to almost 1000 in 1981 and then down to 638 in 1985 and 906 in 986 and up to 1018 in 1987. The upward trend continued in 1988-1989 with harassments up 41 percent and vandalism 19 percent reaching a total of nearly 1300 incidents. These include arsons, cemetery desecrations, anti-Semitic graffiti, threats, and harassments. Some of the more serious vandalism incidents were perpetuated by members of neo-Nazi youth gangs called "Skinheads" in several cities, including Chicago, San Diego, Los Angeles, and Miami. While Vandalism involving hate groups had accounted for no more than 1 or 2 incidents over the past several years, the number jumped to about 20 in 1987. There has also been an increase of anti-Semitic incidents on college campuses in 1988 into 1989: drawing of Swastikas at Yale University, the State University of New York at Binghamton, and Memphis State University; an attack against a Yeshiva University student in Manhattan by a gang of youths shouting anti-Semitic epithets as they beat, robbed and stabbed the 19 year old; and a depiction of Dart mouth colleges Jewish President, James Freedman, by a conservative college newspaper, "Dartmouth Review" as another Hitler. When evaluated in the context of the growth of such other extremist groups as the Ku Klux Klan, the Liberty Lobby, the Aryan Nations, the Posse comitatus, Willis Carto's Liberty Lobby, Lyndon La Rouches organization, and a number of pseudoreligious groups such as the Sword and the Christian Patriot's Defense League, we may be witnessing the beginning of a trend. The guilt feelings felt by many non- Jews concerning the Holocaust may be disappearing.

This is consistent with a growing amnesia about the Holocaust that has taken various forms. As indicated, neo-Nazi tendencies have erupted in western Europe, Canada and the United States. Books in the United States, Britain and France as well as other countries, have denied or minimized the reality of the Holocaust. The publication of Arthur Butz's" The Hoax of the Twentieth century" in

1976, the launching of the Institute for Historical Review in the late 1970s and it's sophisticated journal, the "Journal of Historical review in 1980, were designed to earn scholarly and academic acceptance for revisionism.

This amnesia has shown itself in other ways as well, such as public apathy concerning unpunished war criminals as the controversial invitation by Chancellor Helmutt Kohl to President Ronald Reagan to visit the German military cemetery at Bitburg, where members of the waffen SS lay buried.

So, there are some dark clouds that punctuate the brighter horizon. Conditions for Jews in America have certainly improved since world war II and anti-Semitism has subsided generally, although it has not disappeared completely. America is different than Europe, but it is not different enough. To be sure, Jews are more fully, accepted in American society than ever before, but still there are areas of inequality, there still is ideologicaly based anti-Semitism and stereotyping, and there are the new troubling specters of a Holocaust revisionism and an ideologically motivated anti-Zionism that wishes to strip Jews of their particularity, their history, and their right to self-determination in a world that has too often demonstrated it's tragic indifference.

F. Assimilation:

There are few terms in the vocabulary of ethnicity and ethnic groups, and especially that of Jews, that evoke as many emotions and debates as that of assimilation. It stands to reason that any self conscious ethnic group that strives to survive either as a a minority group within a dominant society and culture or even as an ethic group within a pluralistic society and culture will undertake efforts to resist the tendency for members for that group to lose their identity and identification with the ethnic group. Assimilation is popularly conceived of as unidimensional process within which the members of the ethnic and /or religious group totally blend in with the larger society and culture and cease to consider themselves as part of the ethnic group, but research indicates that the process is much more complex.

With regard to the American Jewish community, the major concern regarding assimilation hinges on its future vis- a -vis the question of intermarriage. But the issue of intermarriage is complex because it involves a variety of subsets of questions, many of which are ideologically laden. The one empirical matter upon which there is consensus is that the rate of intermarriage has risen sharply during the past quarter of a century. Until the early 1960s, American Jews were characterized as an overwhelmingly endogamous group, that is, the overwhelming majority of Jews married Jews. Since then, while precise data are for a variety of reasons, difficult to obtain, the available evidence suggests that nationally, approximately 30 percent of all Jews marry non-Jews. However, this figure is deceptive because it obscures wide regional variations. For example, the intermarriage rate is lower in the creator New York city area that it is in Los Angeles, and it is highest in Denver, where it reaches well over 50 percent. Even with this in mind, what the increase in the intermarriage rate means both quantitatively and qualitatively, is the crux of the disagreement. .

There are two basically different types of intermarriage, namely, mixed marriage and conversionary marriage, which apparently have very different consequences. In the former, the non-Jewish spouse remains non-Jewish, whereas in the latter, the original non-Jewish spouse converts to Judaism. The available evidence strongly suggests that the levels of Jewish ritual practice are substantially higher in conversionary Jewish households than in mixed-marriage house holds. However, we do not have the longitudinal studies that are necessary to determine the impact of having both Jewish and non-Jewish relatives, such as grandparents, uncles, aunts, and first cousins, upon children of even conversionary intermarried couples. We do not know how having non-Jewish close relatives affects these children's own sense of Jewish identity nor do we know whether, in the future, they will continue to identify as Jews. After all, the fact that half 'of the family of a child of an inter-married couple is not Jewish gives that child an option that is unavailable to the child of an endogamous couple. The child of the inter-married couple, therefore, has a much greater degree of freedom to choose not to identify as a Jew. To what extent such children will exercise that option remains to be seen.

From a strictly demographic perspective, the impact of intermarriage is largely dependent upon the proportion of conversionary marriages among all intermarriages. This is so because all of the available data indicate that it is extremely rare for American Jews to overtly leave the Jewish group. Apostacy, in which case the Jew converts to another religion, appears to be minimal, and even cases of defection from the Jewish population without joining another religion appear statistically insignificant. However, as the Israeli demographers Uziel Schmelz and Serglio Delia Pergola point out, the data may be biased because they inherently omit those ex-Jewish men and, probably even more commonly, women who live in non-Jewish neighbourhoods behave in non-Jewish ways, or in other ways manage to evade the researchers conducting population studies for Jewish communal organizations.

Assuming that, in any case, the rate of defection from the Jewish population is low, intermarriage need not spell decline if there is a high rate of conversion to Judaism. If a large proportion of the formerly non-Jewish spouses convert to Judaism, not only is there no inevitable demographic loss; there may well be a gain. The optimists, such as Calvin Goldscheider, convey the general impression that the rate of conversion to Judaism in intermarriages has increased and that now perhaps even more than 50 percent of intermarried couples raise their children as Jews. Charles Silber Man argues even more strongly that intermarriage does not pose a threat to Jewish continuity in America. He strongly argues that if even only half of the children of intermarriages are raised as Jews, there will be no net reduction in the size of the Jewish population, no matter how high the intermarriage rate is, and he, too, argues that the evidence indicates an increasing tendency for intermarried couples to raise their children as Jews.

With respect to Goldscheider's assertion of an increasing levelof conversion, however, a number of studies paint a rather different picture. Their data indicate that not only is the conversion rate not increasing; it is decreasing. For example, in Greater Los Angeles, the second largest Jewish population center is not only in the United states but in the world. Neil Sandberg found that mixed marriages outnumber conversionary marriages among all Jewish intermarriages by there to one. The rate of mixed marriage increases by generation form 11.6 percent among first generation American Jews to 43.5 percent among those in the fourth generation. Both types of intermarriage are related to religious affiliation, with the rates varying from 8.3 percent for the orthodox, 20 percent for the conservative, 37.7 percent for reform, to a high 66.7 percent of the unaffiliated of the fourthgeneration. In addition, Sandberg found a higher rate ofintermarriage in remarriages. Given the rising divorce and remarriage rates of America's Jews, it is likely that the intermarriage rates will rise even higher.

Sandberg's is not the only study to find such patterns. Bruce Phillip's studies of Jewish communities on the west coast (1984) also found that the proportion of mixed marriages among all intermarriages is rising rather than declining, as Goldescheider suggests. In Denver, for example, the percentage or intermarried households rises from 53 percent among those ages 30-39 to 72 percent among those ages 18-29, and the percentage of conversionary households among the intermarried households decreases from 25 percent among those ages 30-39 to 9 percent those ages 18-29. Similar patterns were also found in Phoenix with the percentage of intermarried households increasing from 43 percent to 72 percent and the percentage of conversionary households among intermarried households decreasing from 40 percent to 17 percent between the 30-39 and 18-29 age Cohorts.

Nor are such patterns limited to the west coast. Although the percentages are definitely smaller, similar patterns manifest themselves in Philadelphia (1984) as well. The percentage of intermarried households there increases from 27 percent among those age 30-39 to 38 percent among those ages 18-29, and the percentage of conversionary households among intermarried households decreases from 16 percent among those 30-39 to 12 percent among those 18-29. If patterns such as these are characteristic of the national American Jewish trends, there is a sound basis for questioning the optimism of what has been termed "the new Jewish sociology".

On the other hand, as the optimists point out, intermarriage is not an isolated variable. The extent to which intermarriage is indicative of the decline of the community is also related to the response of the community to intermarriage. Until recently, it was accepted as axiomatic that Jews who intermarry have rejected the Jewish community and their intermarriage is their final step in leaving that community. The new Jewish sociology argues that this most frequently is not the case. Conditions have changed, they argue, and many, if not most of those who intermarry do so for reasons unrelated to their feelings about being Jewish or the Jewish community. They marry for love or other reasons, and at the time of their marriage, they do not consider their Jewishness to be a problem. It is only later, usually when they have children, that the Jewish issues arises. When it does arise, they frequently find that the Jewish community is unwilling to accept them. Their subsequent alienation from the Jewish community, so the argument goes, was not of their own doing. For example, on the basis of his analysis of studies of the Boston Jewish community, Goldscheider (1985) argues that he did not find any ideological basis for intermarriage that favors out-marriages among Jews.

Nor did he find any evidence that intermarriage reflects values that emphasize assimilation. The young Jews in their studies those in their late teens and early twenties do not see a significant connection between intermarriage and total assimilation, he claims. If alienation from the Jewish community does occur it is a consequence of the Jewish community's unwillingness to accept them.

Both the reality of the sharp rise in intermarriage and this new perspective on the social psychology of intermarriage have sparked major policy changes within the organized American Jewish community. It is, today, extremely rare to find the Traditional Jewish rites of mourning being practiced by the families of those who intermarry. The only organized communal refusal to accept intermarriage is that of the relatively small Syrian Jewish community, which has a firm policy prohibiting any conversion, no matter how sincere the particular individual involved might be so that no member of that community even thinks that his or her intermarriage might ever be accepted. Aside from this rare exception, no similar explicit organized communal action exists. All of the religious branches of American Judaism have to one degree or another, adopted a stance that David Singer has characterized as "living with intermarriage".

Reform Judaism has taken the most explicit and dramatic steps to deal with intermarriage. It first adopted as policy a proposal to embark on a major outreach campaign to encourage the conversion of the non-Jewish spouses among intermarried couples. While no such 'de jure' formal policy has been adopted by either conservative or orthodox Judaism, several conservative and Modern Orthodox rabbis have recently written articles urging that traditional Judaism change its stance from one that discourages toward one that encourages conversion. Increasingly, however it is 'de facto' policy of most conservative and orthodox rabbis to encourage conversion among mixed marriage couples.

The second major step of Reform Judaism in this regard was the adoption of a new criterion, at least in terms of the last 2000 years, of determining Jewish status. Whereas traditional Judaism has historically defined a Jew as one born of the Jewish mother or one who converted to Judaism, Reform Judaism's policy of partrilineal descent now recognizes as a Jew the child of either a Jewish mother or a Jewish father, providing the child wishes to so be recognized. The objective of this new policy is to keep the children of intermarried couples intact and within the community.

Although there has been substantial criticism of this policy of patrilineal descent from both the conservative and orthodox rabbinic bodies, in addition to some dissent from within the central conference of American Rabbis (Reform) itself, there has been no major joint effort to rescind it, and the whole issue has largely vanished from the organizational agendas of those rabbinic organizations. Ironically, the only place where it is still a priority issue for some is in Israel, where it is part of the broader struggle over the 'who is a Jew" issue.

Although, as suggested earlier, intermarriage is the major issue of contention between those who perceive assimilation and those who perceive transformation, it is not the only issue. The transformationists point to the fact that the vast majority of respondents in survey after survey report some degree of participation in both religious and communal Jewish activities. If indentificational assimilation were taking place. They argue, the data ought to show much larger number of totally una^ffiliated and unidentified among the respondents. That they do not, the transformationists argue, is clear evidence the assimilationists are wrong. They may be wrong because they are blinded by their own ideologies for example Israeli Zionists and orthodox rabbis have an ideological vested interest in defining any behavior that deviates from that which their ideologies define as proper as assimilation. Even if they have no vested interest in depicting assimilation, they may be simply misled by communal leaders who use their own high standard of communal involvement as the standard and are, thus, unrealistic in their expectations of the involvement levels of the masses. This is especially true with respect to those who derive their predictions of the future based upon the present involvement levels of the youth and young adults of today. What such forecasters frequently overlook is the fact the young adults have a much lower rate of communal participation then others and that rate changes significantly once the young adults become parents. Rather, the transformationists argue, there are many signs of not only enduring but increasing Jewish vitality in American society. These signs may be different than the previous ones, the expression of Jewishness through religious forms is on the decline -but there are many alternative modes of Jewish expression. Greater involvement with Israel, though reading, organizations, and visiting there, is perhaps the clearest manifestation of this phenomenon over the tranformationists.

Others, however, are unconvinced by these arguments. Social scientists with such varied backgrounds and perspectives on other issues as Herbert Gans, Nathan

Glazer, and Charles Liebman are virtually agreed in their skepticism with respect to the ability of America's Jews to withstand the forces of assimilation. Glazer is the most ambivalent, in that he sees merit in the arguments of both the transformationists and the assimilationists. Gans, viewing the whole question within the context of the sociology of ethnicity, sees contemporary American Jewish ethnicity as but: "symbolic ethnicity" an ethnicity that is "worn very lightly" and thus, implicity, probably will not endure for more than several generations.

Perhaps the strongest critic of the transformation and its perspective is Charles Liebman. He is unpersuaded by the argument that new forms of identification have replaced the religious ones because he does not believe that Jewish life can be measured independent of Judaism. In fact, Steven Cohen's own data (1985) as well as those from Paul Ritlerband's study of the Jews of New York city, (1985) indicate that there is a direct correlation between ritual observance and support for Israel as well as with involvement in other forms of Jewish expression.

In addition, Liebman puts little faith in survey research as a means for assessing the vitality of American Jewish life because of a variety of problems associated with the representativity of and the it erpreting of data derived from questionnaires.

Although there are a variety of signs of Jewish revival in American society, they do not necessarily apply to the majority of American Jews. Thus, while a minority is experiencing invigorated Jewish life, the trend for the majority is in the opposite direction. Jews may not be disappearing biologically but, Liebman avers, the quality of Jewish life is obviously eroding and the sociologists of American Jewry ought to formulate their projections more precisely to make this clear. There has been one empirical study designed to test the validity of the two contrasting perspectives. As part of a survey of Jews in New York, Steven cohen (1988) included categories of questions designed to measure the changes over time in various dimensions of Jewishness and Jewish involvement. Those findings do not resolve, however the debate between the perspectives conclusively. There are portions of the findings that lend credence to the assimilationists perspective, other portions that lead in the direction of the transformationist perspective and large portions that suggest that both of these perspectives may be extremes. Rather, a more moderate pattern that is neither clearly assimilationist nor clearly transformationist may be the reality. In any case, the whole issue is far from resolved and only serves to highlight the difficulties of prediction in the social sciences.

G. Problems and prospects:

The sociological realities of the 1908s, with the other movements becoming more militant and most Jews not affiliating with any religious movements have made conservative Judaism in recent years more assertive-communally, legally and theologically.

On a communal basis, conservative leaders are now insisting on the leadership positions in Jewish communal finding for conservative and projects commensurate with conservative numbers. That was not the case previously in part because the strength of the movement made it unnecessary and in part because of a reticence to cause controversy within the Jewish community. The conservative community now has more financial needs; however, as it attempts, in an environment of declining rates of affiliation and rising numbers of new day schools, to maintain Synagogues, train new personnel, and create new materials and programs. .

Some of this new assertiveness grows out of the sense that conservative Judaism has a distinctive, and correct, approach to being Jewish 'in the modern' age and that it has been too meek in promoting its. Its committee on Jewish law and standards no longer is intimidated by the Orthodox or the reform in making what it considers to be approximate decisions in Jewish law that are both traditional and modern. Its rulings on the role of women in Judaism are probably the most well known, but the topics it has touched range the whole gamut of moral, ritual, and communal issues, including matters' of birth and burial, medical ethics and copyright, the Sabbath and dietary law. A mark of this new confidence is the plan to organize and publish the committee's decisions on an ongoing basis so that rabbis can consult them readily and use them in classes and discussions with their congregants. Conservative Jewish law is coming out in the open.

And this is true because of a new assertiveness and openness in theology, with the major exception of mordecai M. Kaplan, conservative thinkers rarely published works regarding matters of belief until the 1950s, in part, probably, because they feared that spelling out the theological implications of the historical approach to Jewish law and tradition would undermine the whole system. Since then, however, writers affiliated with the conservative movement have published a spate of creative theology.

An atmosphere of open inquiry combined with commitment to Jewish law and community have become the distinguishing marks of conservative Judaism as it continues to develop a modern, traditional form of Judaism.

H. Reconstructionism:

A religious ideology and a fourth movement that has emerged in the twentieth century American Jewish life, Reconstructionism was initiated by the teaching and writing of Rabbi Mordecai M. Kaplan. Reconstructionism views Judaism as the involving religious civilization of the Jewish people and seeks, therefore, to adapt inherited Jewish belief and practice to the needs of the contemporary world. It was initially a school of thought that sought to influence and bring together the existing Jewish movements.

The beginning of recontructionism can be dated to 1922 when Kaplan founded the Society for the Advancement of Judaism (SAJ), a synagogue in New York City. At the SAJ, Kaplan developed his approach to Judaism with a group of Jews who were disaffected with other forms of Judaism but committed to reconstructing it in a way that spoke meaningfully in the twentieth century. The congregation experimental with change; in the traditional liturgy, with the inclusion of women, including the introduction of the "bar mitzvah" ceremony in 1922, and with the "revalution" of the Jewish ritual. Jewish intellectuals from all sectors gathered to hear. Kaplan's sermons and talks, in which he continued to develop his new interpretation of Judaism.

Kaplan was first to observe that the Jewish crisis of modernity is a direct result of the loss of social and cultural circumstances socially, since the beginning of the nineteenth century, Jews in various place have undergone political emancipation that has granted them citizenship as individuals in their nations of residence. They participate fully in the surrounding society and thus now have a choice their ancestors lacked about whether and how to identify and participate as Jews. Halakah is no longer the law by which they are governed, and it is therefore no longer functional as a legal system. Thus, a new mode for establishing community norms is needed, one that does not depend on the authority of rabbinic decisions.

Culturally, the world view accepted in the societies in which Jews now live is no longer supportive of traditional Jewish teachings. In its belief in natural causes, modern science undercuts traditional supernaturalism. The primacy of individual autonomy conflicts with the traditional virtue of obedience to Mitzvot and of following communal norms. The teachings of democracy make Jews reluctant to have decisions made by those with authority of Halakic learning. Ecumenicism renders archaic traditional notions of separation and chosenness. Secularism renders counterintuitive the traditional view that God's presence is everywhere. Because Jews are fully integrated into their surrounding cultures, Kaplan thus argued that many traditional teachings required reconstruction if they were to continue to influence the hearts and minds of Jews.

The view of God entails a rejection of the traditional belief that the Torah and its subsequent interpretations are literally divinely revealed, thus eliminating the belief that all the Mitzvoth are God's Commandments and that Jews are rewarded and punished for their level of obedience. The rationale for ritual observance is found rather in the civilization definition of Judaism. Since Jewish civilization is the result of the collective guest of Jews through the generations to live a godly life, Jewish texts, insights, values and practices are of inestimable value to any Jews or Jewish community on a similar quest. And since insights and values cannot be acquired or transmitted as abstract, disembodied principles, Jews can best mine the 'treasures of Jewish tradition by entering the Jewish Universe through ritual practice and study of traditional texts. By thus structuring their lives to see the world through Jewish lenses, they gain access to cultural, psychological, and spiritual treasures that are largely absent from secular western culture.

While there is much in Jewish tradition worthy of recovery, there is also a great deal that requires reconstruction based on contemporary criteria. The Reconstructionists motto here is "Tradition has a vote but not veto." For example, based on the moral value of equality, it is imperative to include women in roles and practices from which they have been excluded by Jewish law.

Culturally, the traditional supernaturalists rationales for most rituals and prayers must undergo what Kaplan termed "revaluation" explaining the meaning of a practice in contemporary terms. Thus, while Sabbath rest was described as a foretaste of the world to come", Jews today ought to observe it as an expression of the ultimate value of spiritual rest in a goat oriented world; while Jews may not believe literally in God's supernatural rescue of the Israelites from Egyptian slavery, the celebration of a revaluated Passover serves as an opportunity to stress the transcendent importance of contemporary meanings of freedom.

Socially, the traditional Jewish emphasis on separation from non-Jews runs counter to the desirable reality of life in the post-Emancipation west. Thus, observance of Kashrut, for example, may sometimes require modification when strict adherence to traditional norms obstructs important social intercourse.

Kaplan advocated a process of collective study of traditional sources and their rationales for mitzoth so that communities could reach norms for public practice together. In line with this approach, each Reconstructionist is individually and communally engaged in study and experimentation with the aim of incorporating an increasing level of ritual observance into his or her daily life. As a result, the degree of Jewish study and ritual practice among Reconstructionists tends to be high.

Because a nonsupernaturalistic God could not literally choose one people over another and because the claim of privileged access to God promotes, however unintentionally, odious feelings if superiority Kaplan sought to dispense with the idea that the Jewish people are chosen by God, going so far as to eliminate all references to chosenness from the liturgy. In traditional Jewish caching, this teaching had, in large part, focused on the superiority of Torah rather than on the distinctiveness of Jews, When it is adopted however, by Jews who do not accept the revealed, binding nature of the Commandments, it is transformed into an undersirable chauvinism.

For Jewish civilization to thrive in the modern world, Kaplan believed that the traditional, preemancipation community would have to be reconstituted. He proposed and advocated the formation of an organic community a super-Kehillah to nurture the development of functioning Jewish communities in North America. The community, which Jews would join by payment of dues, would include all religious and secular Jewish organizations and would have a monopoly on providing Jewish services life cycle rituals Kosher food, worship services, social and educational programs.

Conclusion: -

The location of Jewish culture lies in the above mentioned factors. The novel "The Victim" by Saul Bellow and "Shosha" by I.B. Singer is based on all these factors. In the next chapter the location of culture in Saul Bellow's, "The Victim" is discussed.

Notes:

1) Ed. Procter Paul,
   Longman Dictionary of Contemporary English P. No. 270. Longman Group Limited. Pub. 1978.:)
2) Ibid P. No. 228.
3) BhabhaK. Homi P. No. 1.
   The location of culture: London and New York.
4) Ibid P. No. 3.
5) Ibid P. No. 4.
6) Ibid P. No. 9.
7) Kazin Alfred: "Though He Slay Me", Pg. No. 3.
8) Jewish American History and Culture; An Encyclopedia. Vol. 429. P. No. 30.

Chapter - II

LOCATION OF CULTURE IN SAUL BELLOW'S THE VICTIM

A) About the author, Saul Bellow:-

In 1941 he published his first short story "Two Morning Monologues", in Partisan Review "Dangling Man" his first novel was published in 1944. *"The Victim" his second novel was published in 1947. In 1953 he published his third novel, "The Adventures of Augie March", and won the National Book Award for "The Adventures of Augie March" in 1954. In 1956, he published "Seize the Day".

In 1975 he published "Humboldt's Gift". 1976 was remarkable year in the life of Saul Bellow. He won the Pulitzer Pirze for literature for "Humboldt's Gift", published "To Jerusalem and Back: A personal Account" and received Nobel Prize for literature in the same year.

Bellow Saul, The Victim, Penguin Books, 1947. All subsequent references to the text are from this edition.

Contemporary American fiction as exemplified by the novels of Saul Bellow, Norman Mailer, Bernard Malamud and Salinger in particular seems to explore, rather then to assess, unexampled territiories of life, it's contradictions and anamolies. It is not so much concerned with social defeats and victories as with its "adamic falls and quixotic redemptions". But on the contrary, as Jonathan Baunbach has pointed out, it seeks to examine, "by the large the shadow landscape of the self, often in the disguise of a dimly recognizable "real" world-a Mythic world more consequential than the one it pretends to represent, more believable and horrible, more possible to survive in"[1] Stemming from a disinterested study of experience, the American novel relatively is free from the pseudo technical virtuosity, which tends to vitiate much of recent fiction.

The ability to embody the complexity of life to rise to what Allen Tate has called the "complexity of feeling", which "from Hawthorne down to our time has baffled our best understanding".[2] This complexity of feeling is obvious from the opposition in American experience between "tradition and progress".... between liberalism and conservatism, aggressive acquisitive economics and benevolent wealth."[3] Generally speaking, it may also be due to ours being a self conscious age and man fast losing touch with his own world while, paradoxically enough, being on the verge of conquering other being on the verge of conquering other worlds. Historically speaking, the same divisions were in vogue in Europe also, but they were contained by a closer social medium, a valid, richer sense of the past, and a more realistic sense of material possibilities. There is an undoubted disparity, as Tocqueville has suggested, between innocence and experience thought and action, ideal and practice. It is from this disparity that the tendency of the American mind to oscillate wildly between ideas that are "all either extremely minute and clear or extremely general and vague" stems. For literary efforts this meant a fusion which results from "a struggle to close the split in American experience, to discover a unity that, for the artist especially, almost was not there".[4]

These contradictions, however are traceable partly, to certain historic facts. First, there is the solitary position of man in America, a position enforced by the "doctrines of Puritanism by the very institutions of democracy" as revealed in the 18th and 19th centuries. Second, the Manichaen quality of New England Puritanism with its tenets of "election and damnation, its opposition of the Kingdom of light and the kingdom of darkness, its eternal and autonomous contraries of good and evil"[5]- has caputred the Manichean sensibility. A third source of contraction lies in the dual allegiance of the American who intellectually belong both to the old world and the new.

All art tends to discover reality and the multiplicity of modern American existence makes this discovery doubly attractive and challenging. While as artists the American writers are bound to strive for the dissolution of all contradictions, as Americans they have the further exciting task of discovery the essential identity submerged under the multiplicity of American life. "The serious novel "says Norman Mailer begins from a fixed philosophical point-the desire to discover reality- and it goes to search for that reality in society or else embark on a strip up the upper Amazon of the inner eyes;"[6] Consequently, American novels either tend to be extremely embarrassing and naive pictures of reality or annoyingly obscure analyses of private symbols and myths. But a rare few have succeeded in fusing both versions of the experience. They have fused self and society in an imaginative vision which assigns these two things to their proper places of these select few in contemporary American fiction Saul Bellow easily occupies a distinct place of his own.

Bellow's work seeks to define the changing face of contemporary American fiction where the hero is usually a meeting point of conflicting values. We see the hero as Ihab Hassan has pointed out, "as actor and sufferer, rebel and victim, rogue and saint"; we see him in the glow of fiction, darkly, paradoxically as man both typical and uncommon the outsider in the street;'"7 'the centrality of vision in Bellow's fiction originates from the same vantage point of contradictory experience. His heroes are caught between the everlasting 'Yes' and the eternal 'No' and seem to live in a state of tension. At the heart of the Bellow hero there is a duality, he yearns for social recognition but is held back by a passionate desire to retain his own identity as an individual. The recognition of social reality is there, but there is also a failure to achieve any meaningful relationship with it. The struggle to achieve this community is the very passion of Bellow's hero, but ironically he is locked up within himself, ''divorced from the world''. This given rise to two mutually but only apparently contradictory tendencies in the Bellow hero. He desperately needs community but the price he has to pay for this is destruction of his own individuality, for Bellow "potrays a community in which the price of admission is destruction."8

Bellow's heroes embody a tension between a man of love and a man of will. This can be ultimately traced to two opposing views of the world; as Keith Michael Opdahl says, "Bellow is torn between his admiration of militant struggle and his insistence upon a less wilful and defenceless, joy."[9] Bellow treats the personal and the social as a continuum in which personality finds justification in a universal principle or moral order, which it reflects. But Bellow gives a further dimension to the traditional American hero by making him embody a religious quest. Bellow's heroes seek a religious and cultural quest which distinguishes them from the protagonists of say, Hemingway, Yeats and Lowell. This explains the protagonists inability to break out of himself. He is unable to reconcile vision with the daily world; although he exists in a carefully defined social context. He suffers from a sense of incompletion of disunity, and yet he seeks some sort of rebirth or redemption. The world is unreal to the protagonist because he denies that he is part of it; seeking to evade limitations of physical existence, he divorces himself from it and thus divorces himself from reality. Bellow is aware of the ultimate helplessness of man before fate. He defines not the resolution of man's conflict with fate but the very spectacle of man seeking resolution[10].

"The Victim" was published and set in 1947, in the postwar era when so many second generation Jewish-Americans, the children of immigrants, the depression and the war now over, were beginning to move up in large members into middle- class, white-collar positions. The location of the culture of the novel is not purely orthodox Jewish. But it is quite modern. Saul Bellow has sketched the novel in the modern American society, which tries to alienate the protagonist because of his Jewishness. There are twenty four chapters in the novel which locate the culture and the conflicts among the Jews who lived in the post-war era in the white - collared American society.

Asa Levanthal, a Jew and editor of a small magazine is temporarily left alone in New York when his wife goes to visit her mother. He is confronted by a remote acquaintance, Kirby Albee, an anti-semite-seedy, unkempt, like "one of those you saw sleeping off their whisky on Third Avenue". A drifting alcoholic, Albee lost a job years ago (soon after Levanthal) and now he blames Levanthal and holds him responsible for his losing his job and this was maliciously done because Albee had once spoken against the Jews. Bellow is a great craftsman, a creative man. He is analyzing Asa Levanthal. He is a prototypical young man like any other young man in the modern society attending to his daily routines and performing his duties as consciously as possible. But he is also living in the world that is characterized by the profit motif and a world that is pre-occupied with notions of utility and usefulness, in this kind of a Utilitarian society, notions of community and family have been rendered redundant, consequently, Asa is caught like a helpless animal between two warring worlds of social duty and commitment to family.

The family is a moral burden from the past that he has to carry on and the social duty is a kind of cross, he must bear to his own crucification. 'His sister - in - law is sentimental, confused and indecisive. She depends on Asa heavily for emotional and moral support, but lacks the sense of propriety.

She rings up Asa in middle of busy office schedule and expects him to quit his office and rush home. Because Asa's brother and her husband is away from house for the purpose of work, she depends heavily for help on Asa. She does not understand the constraints of official duty. To her Asa's presence is emotionally and morally reassuring. This puts Asa in a peculiar situation. His colleagues and co-workers distrust him not as an individual but as a stereotype, a representative of a certain community. And very often he is humiliated indirectly. And his family depends so heavily on him that duty to family is extremely painful and tiring obligation. As a result Asa is confused, nervous, agitated and absent minded. But unfortunately he lacks the resources to fight against the collective ethnic bias against him on one hand and on other he is terrible enfeeble when thrown into family liabilities. Levanthal is an unheroic hero. Asa has big nose bulging eyes, large head i.e., an ugly appearance. His mother died as a mad woman. Asa looks some what like a sub-normal creature.

Asa is very systematically constructed as a young man without a noble family background and with an ironic suggestion, i.e. history of madness in his family. His physical features, dress habits too indicate something abnormal, awakard about Asa levanthal and seen from a conventional perspective, Asa is apparently unheroic. Everything in his form and structure suggest the absence of harmony and balance and even the traditional heroic notions of handsomeness. The intention is obviously to create modern narrative prototype anti-hero.

In most Jewish novels and stories, Jew is very heroic character, with few exceptions, Jew is invariably presented as victim rather than a heroic victimizer. He is not somebody set out to conquer the world or explore the limits of Universe, but somebody who is conquered, constantly changed and constantly harassed. For all practical purposes he has a very limited family. His young brother and his wife Elena. And Asa's career as a young man too is a record of failure and frustration. He takes courses in college, he cannot complete and undertakes assignments beyond his capacity and the painful feeling of doing something incompatible with his nature weighs very heavily on his heart and conscious. In no way he is prince charming who fascinates young girls or or draws attention of future employers and people who matter in business. He spends his time in reading books that are apparently outdated in the modern world. Obviously, this is an unusual and slightly ludicrous image of a hero. None the less, Asa is the centre of the narrative action.

Mary is Asa's wife and Max is his younger brother. In the absence of both, Asa is left all alone. Mary goes temporarily to visit her mother. Max has two sons Mickey and Philip. Mickey dies later in the novel. Leventhal whose mother had died in an insane asylum when he was eight and who has always feared madness in himself and often suspected it in other is nearly broken by the moral and emotional demands placed on him by his excitable, Italian - American sister in - law, Elena and the drunken unstable Allbee.

B) Holocaust and The Victim:

Although Critics have differed on the relationship of "The Victim" to the Holocaust, there is a general consensus that its presence is essentially muffled, it is not significant.

For Mark Schechner, it is "deeply buried, yet tightly woven into the fabric of the narrative rarely explicit but there, like a symptiom". L. H. Goldman notes the curious silence on the topic of Bellow's normally loquacious characters. Peter Hyland argues that despite a focus an anti - Semitism, the novel does not treat the Holcaust directly, though he feels it is "haunted" by it. (P. 23) One of the most recent critics to discuss the novel Michael Glenday, even rejects the importance of anti-semitism to the novel: "I cannot follow the argument of those critics who regard this novel as Centrally concerned with anti-semitism. (P.28) Glenday proceeds to a thorough revision of Allbee who rises proportionately in the critical scale as Leventhal sinks. For Glenday, Leventhal is a Jew without any of the fine Jewish qualities (P.27), "who suffers from touchiness about anti – Semitism" (P.29) and who appears as "Caliban" to Allbee's prospers. An "infirma species" inhabiting a "debased reality" (P.34).

Glenday's view stands in strong contrast to Malcolm Bradbury's "The repulsive Allbee",(P. 40) Tonny Tanner's "anti-semitic" degenerate failure (P. 27) and Ihab Hassan's refreshingly reboust "insufferable Creep" (P. 299-300). Apart from the discussion of anti-semitism only. One critic, S. Lillian Kremer has drawn attention to specific Holocaust material in the novel in it's pervasive images of asphyxiation the color yellow (the badge), and closely packed.

However, the Holcaust provides the occasion and the major structural principle of the novel, particularly in relation to its double plot. Various commentators have noted the motif of Allbee as the double in "The Victim", with influence of Dostoevsky particularly cited (Baumbach, Fuchs). In addition the novel alternates between two plots

Leventhals perseution by anti Semitic Allbee, and the sickness and death of Mickey, Leventhal's brother's child, a plot which is often seen as subordinate to the Allbee story.

First, however, a brief excurses into Saul Bellow's autobiography. In an interview in 1990 Bellow was asked about the relative absence of the Holocaust in his writing. He commented, "There were lots of things I hadn't been able to incorporate. Things that got away from me. The Holcaust for one I may even have been partly sealed off from it" (It all Adds up 312). According to Bellow it was only in 1959 when he visited' Auschwitz, that the Holcaust, he says, "landed it's whole weight on me" (P.313). He admitted to finding it odd that he had not been moved to write about it "I can't interpret it creditably to myself. I am still wondering at it I lost close relatives" (P. 313). Bellow's reluctance to confront the topic- understandable as it is - becomes potentially more comprehensible in the description offered, in the same interview, of his childhood. At the age of eight Bellow spent six months in hospital with tuberculosis. Already a good reader he could read his chart at the end of the bed and knew, even at the age of eight, that it was very unpromising" (P. 289). In the ward he was constantly exposed to the death of children.

> This happened regularly. A lot of fussing in the
> night and screem around the Kind's bed and running
> back and forth with last lights. And in the morning
> an empty bed. You just saw the bed made up for
> another Kid. Before long there was a kid in it. You
> understand very well what had happened, but it
> wasn't discussed or 'explained'. (P.290).

As a result Bellow felt forever after that he had been in some fashion "excused from death" (P. 289) "that it was a triumph that (he') had gotten away with it (P. 289). There was he "concluded," a duty that came with survival" (P 289). "I owned something to a duty that came with "survival" (P.289). "I owned something to some entity for the privilege of surviving" (P.289). Bellow, in short, was already possessed-very early age - of that complex of emotions which William G. Miederland has termed the "survivor syndrome" (Epstein 100-103). In this childish narcissm, Bellow describes his survival as a 'triumph. In the most provocative analysis of the survivor, Elias Canetti argues:

"The moment of survival is the moment of power. Horror at the sight of death turns into satisfaction that it is someone else who is dead... Whether the survivor is confronted by one dead man or by many, the essence of the situation is that he feels unique.. All men's designs on immortality contain something of this desire for survival" (P. 227).

Bellow also describes himself as having got away with it as if he had escaped a deserved punishment, Robert J. Lifton (who studied survivors of Hiroshima & the Holocaust) found "survival guilt" a common phenomenon, a magnification of the guilt that is present in every bereaved person. Why am I-unworthy that I am-alive when better people are not? (Epstein P. 107).

In the Victim, Leventhal is away from the dreadful Holocaust. His imagery here draws upon the notion of economic disaster but his guilt is clearly that of a survivor who did not particularly deserve to survive, but was luckier than the rest. The 'slippage here between economic and historical frames of reference has a special relevance to Bellow's reaction to the Holocaust. In an interview, Bellow was asked about the intellectual impact of the Second World War. He replied that he had completely misunderstood the war because he was under the influence of Marxism. Although Kristall Nacht gave him pause, Bellow as a Trotskyist, stood by the belief that a worker's state; however degenerate, could not wage an imperialist war." I was still at that time offically sold on Marxism and revolution but sobered up when France fell" (P. 307). The Victim is Bellow's examination of both the guilt and the responsibilities of the survivor. It is, in a sense, about the Holocaust, because it is not ostensibly, about the Holocaust.

> It is related of auspicious king, that there was a
> merchant of the merchants who had much wealth,
> and business in various cities. Now on a day he
> mounted horse and went forth to recover monies
> in certain towns, and the heat oppressed him; so he
> sat beneath a tree and putting his hand into his
> saddle- bags he took thence some broken bread and
> dried dates and began to break fast. When he had
> ended eating the dates he threw away the stones with
> force and lo ! an Ifrit appeared huge of sature and
> brandishing a drawn sword wherewith he
> approached the merchant and said," stand up that I
> amy slay thee even as thoug slewest my son !"
> Asked the merchant", How have I slain they son?'
> and he answered 'when thoua test dates and

therewest away the stones they struck my son full
in the breast as he was walking by, so that he died
forewith? (The Tale of the Trader and the Jinni, from
thousand & one nights.) (Epigraph to The Victim)
"Be that at it may, now it was that upon the
rocking waters of the ocean the human face began
to reveal itself; the sea appeared paved with
innumerable faces, upturned to the heavens' faces,
imploring, wrathful, despairing; faces that surged
upward by thousands, by myriads, by generations.-

- De Quincey
The Pains of Opium. (P. 1)

These epigraphs to the novel strike the appropriate
note. The first in which a merchant accidentally kills the
child of an Ifrit and is promptly faced with massive and
apparently undeserved retribution, could hardly offer a
more telling example of undeserved guilt. The accidental
nature of the death (Ifrit's frits, child is killed by a
discarded date stone) corresponds to that of Mickey, an
innocent killed by an extremely rare bronchial infection,
a death for which nobody, certainly not Leventhal - can
be blamed. The second epigraph offers a more disquieting
image of a multiplication of the individaul as frightening &
connecting. In "The Pains of Opium", De Quincy precedes
this image of a mob of persecutors concealed behind one
face with lines which emphasize the presence in his dreams
of "the tyranny of the human face", with its "tormenting"
powers (P. 137). De Quincy's mental disturbances have been
traced, persuasively, to the death of a child, his young sister,
whose bandaged head created in De Quincy a morbid fear of

turbans and thus of the East (Barrel). His night mares were full of oriental and Asian images, and he was particularly tormented by the figure of a Malay who had visited him at words worth's cottage in Grasmere and who, in his opium addiction, assumed the role of demonic double.' De Quincy gave the Malay enough opium to kill him on the spot, but the double survived to haunt him in his dreams. After the passage which Bellow quotes, De Quincy continues, "The Malay has been a fearful enemy for months. I have been every night through his means, transported into Asiatic scenes" (P. 137) and we turn we turn the page to find that Bellow's novel begins, "on some nights New York is as hot as Bangkok"(P.2) going on to evoke a composite orientatlist scenes of tropical heat and foliage and barbaric fellahin". The two epigraphs initiate a novel in which death, responsibility, guilt, racial prejudice the emergence of a persecuting double, all combine.

It is important to note here that it is only after the onset of Mickey's serious illness that Allbee puts in an appearance. Indeed, according to Elena, Mickey has died and revived. When Leventhal is called to his sickbed, Elena tells him that Mickey had stopped breathing for a period. Leventhal corrects her "He was breathing all the time. How could he stop and start again?"(P. 6) but she insists that he did. Leventhal's reaction is extreme: Leventhal's composure was not perfect; it was tinged with fear. He thought," what superstition! just like in the old country. The dead can come back to life, too, I suppose and all the rest of it" (P. 6). Writing about the uncanny, Freud explicitly connected it with "that class of the frightening which leads back to what is known of old and long familiar" (P. 220).

Now it is obvious that Bellow's novel offers a multiplicity of points to show the effects of Holocaust. Mickey's death hangs over the action, filling Leventhal with fear. Allbee returns to haunt him after years of absence - Leventhal has repressed all memory of him. His uncanny nature is dramatized in his mysterious appearance. Leventhal hears a bell ring - but there is nobody at the door, not has the super seen anyone enter or leave. Yet Allbee's letter is in Leventhal's box. Again a background featuring a revivalist band Allbee appears in a line next to a chorous girl, a heavily painted lady whose significance is connected to commodified replication (the identical members of a chorus line)

Allbee appears as a ghastly harbinger of death and a persecuting double in direct response to the threat to Mickey. Just as the Holocaust reactivated Bellow's childhood experience, reviving repressed material in sharpened guilty form so in the novel, a Jewish child is threatened by death, and in guilt and fear Leventhal allows a double to emerge to persecute him. Allbee is repeatedly characterized by Leventhal as a bad actor, a poor imitation of the genuine article - himself. The horror film which Leventhal attends in the novel also highlights the uncanny double; "an old scientist was seen haunting the dressing room of a theatre where he had murdered his mistress many years ago. He had hallucinations about a young star who resembled her and he attempted to strangle the girl "(P. 91). The climax" (1944), lavishly filmed in the Paris Opera, which marks Boris Karloffs return to Hollywood after his rejection of monster roles in favor of more "dignified" ones (Jensen 133). Karloff plays a physician who has killed a singer and now finds that the new start is the double of her predecessor.

Leventhal finds himself unable to watch the film which takes place in a deathly environment a stifling airless cinema with "nebulous" lamps in "dusteaten" shades (P. 92). When he goes out for air, however, he is confronted by an old man who describes Karloff as understanding" what a Mastermind is, a law unto himself (P. 92). The old man's description of total narcissitic involvement irresistibly recalls the Nazi glorification of the Superman or Uber mensch. Jung, indeed, argued that the appeal of Hitler rested on his ability to function as the shadow (Jung's term for the alter ego) to the entire German people (P. 6).

If the film connects acting doubles and the Holocaust, the subsequent cafeteria discussion of what constitutes good acting is no less relevant as a group of Jews argue about anti Simitism and acting (in the double senses of role play and moral behavior) Schlossberg's test for a good actor is the appropriate response to death. His examples involve the bereaved Nazimova, as one of Chekhov's "Three sister", and Livia Hall (close homophone to Leventhal) as the murderess of her "other half. The group speculate about acting as duplication wondering, for example why mere are "so many victorias" (P. 117). Later in the novel Shlossberg reappears, still discussing death, in this case the modern inability to face it, as opposed to an older generation that can converse ranges over insurance against death (in the economic not the psychological sense), the sewing of one's own shroud, and survival guilt. (Mrs. Harkavy feels "wicked still to be here at my age while the children die" (P. 204) Schlossberg draws the moral.

"I have to be myself in full. Which is somebody
who dies, isn't it?..... I am not three people, four
people. I was born once and I will die once. You
want to be two people? More than human? Maybe
it's because you don't know how to be one. (P. 212)

Schlossberg goes on to lament the transformation of
modern man into a whole corporation of selves, replicating
the division of labor most critics have read the image of
the crowed in "The Victim" in similarly economic terms
as representing the pressures of urban life and the masses
(Bradbury 40-47). As Bellow's De Quincy epigraph suggests
however, and as the pushing stifling crowds in the novel
confirm the crowd also features as an image of a number
of replica selves hostile and competitive, an image of
destruction by and in the mass. When Leventhal takes the
ferry from Mickey's sickbed back to New York for example,
he finds himself amidst a "crowd of souls" (P. 61).

The images of crowds, acting and the Holocaust come
together in two dreams. The first of them occurs when
Leventhal has finally allowed Allbee into his home, despite
the fact that Allbee is clearly bent on prersecuting him
and has wrung from him the only overt reference of the
Holocaust in the novel. "Millions of us have been killed"
(P. 127). Beginning as a response to the fear of death,
Allbee has become the double who punishes Leventhal for
surviving, making him relive the experiences of anti-Semitic
persecution. In the dream, Leventhal is quite overtly split
into two selves. "He had an unclear dream in which he held
himself off like an unwilling spectator yet it was he that
did everything" (P. 142). The situation, a railway station

hung with flags, in which crowds controlled by guards are being loaded onto trains, is instantly recognizable as an image of the Holocaust (Kremer). Leventhal however is eager to board the train, running in an attempt to catch it. A surge of the crowd displace him into a freshly paved and plastered corridor, a new installation, but before he can reach the tracks, he is halted by two men. The one a working man, appears sympathetic but "he was an 'employee and couldn't interfere" (P. 143). (He is only following orders. The other, in a business suit, pushes Leventhal out into an alley. Leventhal's face is covered with tears. The dream suggests that Leventhal has made every effort - in his double dream self to get on the crowd around him, but has been thwarted despite himself.

Waking, Leventhal has "a sense of marvellous relief... a rare pure felling of happiness" (P. 139). His dream double has assuaged his guilt, sought out his own destruction, and been excused from death by a mysterious authority figure. Leventhal has a sudden insight; "It was supremely plain to him that everything, everything without exception took place as if within a single soul or person (P. 139). Fragmentation yields to unity here, in the reverse of the opening epigraph, as the self comes back together and the threatening mass becomes a single soul. One is reminded of the American motto "E Pluribus Unum" one out of many Leventhal, of course, escaped the fate of European Jewry because he was in America.

After Mickey's death, as Leventhal accepts that he is one person, a person who dies, his relation to the crowd changes. In the park after Mickey's funeral he hears the revivalist band and remembers a story he had once read abut "hell cracking open... and all the souls, crammed together, looking out" (P. 151). Eyeing the crowd around him, however, he continues, "But these were alive, this young couple., this woman late in pregnancy" (P. 151) Despite his sorrow, Leventhal is now able to accept death's and to turn towards life and love. In allowing Allbee to persecute him he has largely exorcised his excessive guilts and surrendered his narcissistic defenses. Now, "Max and the family replaced Allbee in his mind" (P. 154), and he sends for his wife.

It should come as no surprise therefore that Leventhal's ensuing dream, which also has a bearing on the Holocaust, should include a double but a double firmaly teminized. The dream also returns to the business representatives of the first dream, not as a saviour but as complicit in the horror. In the dream, a salesgirl in a store demonstrates shades of rouge to Leventhal by drawing sports on her face, wiping each off on a soiled hand towel, dyed red as a result, and then bending back 'to the mirror to repeat the process. The salesgirl recalls the painted ladies of Freud's essay on the uncanny (to whom he was repeatedly drawn back), the chorus girl of the earlier scene and (Via the image of stage make up) the notion of acting. In making herself up the woman is "putting on a face" - many face multiplied in the mirror. Leventhal, however, is brought to semi consciousness by the smell of the red soiled towel. (The female symbolism here does not need to be belabored).

The battle is between a woman and an uncanny double. "The odor of the towel had from the begining seemed familiar" (228, my emphasis). The return of the familiar, the repressed marks the return of the Holocaust to consciousness. Leventhal's mind, semicounscious, moves from the towel to the bathroom and to an uneasy awareness that though he can hear steam hissing in the pipes, the room is cold. He rouses himself to the smell of hissing gas: Albee is attempting to gas them both. "Gas was pouring from the oven". (P. 229). The reference to Nazis "shower" could hardly be more explicit. Where Leventhal's first dream potentially suggested the saving force of capitalist America (the business man) the second dream indicts big business, recalling its crucial role in the Holocaust. Bellows' Marxism was not lightly abandoned. The colors (German "Farben") of the woman's paint recall I. G. Farben, the German business conglomerate which began by making dyestuffs, then went on to build both its own new plant and a private concentration camp at Auschwitz and manufactured Zyklon B, the gas for its extermination Llock (a gas deliberately manufactured without the "indicator" of its familar smell). Leventhal's dream began with an image of cars in rapid motion. I. G. Farben made the synthetic gas and rubber on which Nazi Germany depended for its mobility." In the dream. The familiar links to the source of horror; Leventhal's life. however, is saved by his ability to bring the repressed matter to the surface, to consciousness, a consciousness assisted here by the female presence in the dream. The dream expresses Leventhal's renewed - if fearful- openness to sexual love and the disappearance of the deathly double. Allbee is now firmly ejected.

At the close of the novel, several years later the reader learns that Leventhal looks years younger and has "lost the feeling that he had, and he used to say, got away with it" (P. 230). When Allbee reappears at the theatre he looks older, unhealthy with a decayed appearance and deepened wrinkles about his eyes, wrinkles which have "a fabric quality, crumpled and blank. (P.236)- very much the image of the aging or decaying portrait. Appropriately he is in the company of an actress, Yvonme Crane, whose professional existence depends upon defying the ageing process and playing many roles. Mary, who has seen her picture "a hundred times" (P. 134), comments, "How do they stay looking so young?" (P. 234) Leventhal, on the other hand, has accepted a more natural means to immortality Eyeing the pregnant Mary, Allbee comments that Leventhal is clearly following the injection to "increase and Multiply" (P. 236). It is in some ways an inconclusive ending, leaving the reader poised between the hero and the double and ending on a question.

The Victim was therapeutic for Bellow, who himself noted a change after it from gloom to holiday (All Adds up 318). Critics also have been swift to see the subsequent novel.

"The adventures of Augie March" as marking a break through. Bellow's first epigraph is taken from "The Tale of the Trader and the Jinni. This story is an example of the "ransom frame" in which the act of storytelling serves to redeem a human life (Caracciolo). In the story the Merchant is saved by the intervention of two other storytellers whose stories distract the Jinni, much as Scheherazade distracts Shahrriar in the frame-tale from his intention to kill her. In other words the merchant is saved from suffering as a result of a death which he did not intend, by the very process of storytelling. As Paul Coates puts it.:

Works of fiction exist in a space between the Double and other other. To enter into a work of fiction is in a sense to transform the other into a double ; to discover in the apparent foreignness of another person the lineaments of one's own aspirations and hopes. (P. 1) (The Double and the other -Paul Coates)

As the multiple plot structures of the "Thousands and one Nights "demonstrate, storytelling is a better defence against the powers of death than any other, for it doubles reader, author, and character, by sympathetic identification- a form of love." The Victim is a narrative of trauma which becomes a narrative of reparation, the first of long, reparative career.

Arguably, it is also highly suggestive in the paradigm offered for the importance of the theme of death in Bellow's novels and for the treatment there of. Double plots are a common feature of Bellow's writing, with one half of the pair, as in De Quincy, often associated with the "Other". America and Mexico in "The Adventures of Augie March", America and Africa in "Henderson, the Rain King", America and Eastern Europe in "The Dean's December", Dr. Lal in "Mr. Sammler's planet', Dahfu in "Henderson, the Rain King, and the pickpocket in "Mr. Samler's planet." In "Humboldts Gift" Cantabile emerges as a persecuting double when Citrine learns of the death of Humboldt; Henderson sets off for Africa in immediate response to the death of Miss. Lenox; the death of Valeria haunts "The Dean's December"., "Seize the Day" ends with Tommy Wilhelm absorbed into the crowd at a funeral. Herzog writes letters to the dead but is brought back to emotional health after watching the trail of a woman accused of causing the death of a small child. Even more suggestively, in the light of Bellow's ambivalence to his Trots Kyite past, when Augie encounters Trotsky in Mexico, he identifies him with the power of death; "Death discredits. Survival is the whole success. The voice of the dead goes away. There isn't any memory. The power that's established fills the earth and destiny is whatever survives" (P. 482).

More generally, The Victim offers an illuminating comparative perspective on other novels of trauma and mass death. Toni Morrison's "Beloved", for example, with its epigraph, "Sixty million and more" focuses on the uncanny tale of a murdered child returning as a ghostly double to haunt and persecute the guilty mother, coming between mother and lover and finally being ejected only after threatening her life. Louise Erdrich's Tracks' moves from an opening evocation of genocide to the rescue of dying child and a narrative which alternates between two trickster figures, Nanapush and Pauline. As an aged Chippewa trickster figure, Nanapush may seem to have little connection to Saul Bellow's Urban heroes, yet faced with the threat of death he uses the same tactic of storytelling as survival mechanism.

> "During the year of sickness when I was the last
> one left, I saved myself by starting a story... I could
> hardly keep moving my lips. But I did continue and
> recovered. I got well by talking. Death could not
> get a word in edgewise, grew discourage and
> traveled on. (Tracks 46').

C) **Cultural conflict:**

In New York, Asa Leventhal meets with a great misfortune, his nephew's rare disease. Later Kirby Allbee drives him into a tighter corner Allbee appears before Leventhal after a long absence, places the responsibility for his own present wretched plight on him, and follows him like a shadow.

Asa Leventhal undergoes a great cultural conflict. In the very first chapter when he takes the permission from Mr. Beard to go to see his sick nephew on receiving a phone call from Elena, he rudely says.

"Walks out right in the middle of everything. Right in a pinch with everybody else swamped". (P.3) Another voice which he identified as that of Mr. Fay, the business manager, answered.

It's funny that he should just pick up and go. There must be something up". And Mr. Beard continued. (P. 3).

"Takes unfair advantage like the rest of his brethren. I have never known one who wouldn't. Always please themselves first. Why didn't he offer to come back later, at least?"

The view of the non-Jews towards the Jews is explained through the above lines. They are not concerned about Asa's problem or his nephew's sickness, but they feel that he is taking undue advantage of becoming a Jew. Leventhal exchanges not only looks but also voices with others. In other words, Leventhal's consciousness mixes with those of other people around him. Asa Leventhal and his brother, Max are away from each other. There is such a difference between them that Elena, Asa's sister-in-law does not know even the name of Asa's wife, nor Philip, his nephew knows that Asa is his uncle. Bellow has very skillfully sketched the features of a typical Jew in the beginning of chapter no. two;

"Leventhal's figure was burly, his head large; his nose, too was large. He had black hair, coarse waves of it, and his eyes under their intergrown brows were intensely black and of a size unusual in adult faces. But though childishly large they were no childlike in expression. They seemed to disclose an intelligence not greatly interested in it's own powers as if preferring not to be bothered by them, indifferent; and this indifference appeared to be extended to others. He did not look sullen but rather unaccommodating, impassive". (P. 10)

In addition, Leventhal guesses the other's minds he conjectures on Max's Italian - American mother - in- law's view of Mickey's rare disease in a speechless confrontation with her, Philip's state of mind, Allbee's loss of employment seen from "Rudiger's standpoint" (P. 107-108), and Elena's view of the irresponsibility for Mickey's death. Mary, Asa's wife had an affair with a married man before meeting him, which disturbs Asa very much. But after mary's persuasion, they married each other. There is a great feeling of hatred towards the Jews, the Christians hate them vigorously.: chapter no.3 the following lines uttered by Allbee is a good example of this hartred;

"You Jews have funny ideas about drinking. Especially the one that all Gentiles are born drunkards. You have a song about it. "Drunk he is, drink he must, because he is a Goy Schicker". (P.29) Jews oftern feel embarrassed in the company of Christians. As Williston's house, Asa is force to sing a Jewish song, but he feels embarrased because Allbee behaves with him in a quite different manner, "Then any Jewish song. Something you have really got felling for. Sing us the one about the mother. And with a drunken look of expectancy he (Allbee) bent forward, leaning on his knees, and pretended to prepare to listen. It was apparent to everyone that he was deeply pleased; he smiled at Harkary and the girl and he had a glace for Leventhal too. His wife seemed quietly to dissociate herself herself from him. The Willistons were embarrassed. Allbee was not merely an acquaintatnce but a friend, and Willliston later tried to make excuses for him and explain away the insult."

With his consciousness mixed with the other's, Leventhal comes to notice the danger of mental confinement and considers Allbee to be his "double". The others bring Leventhal not only the different views of things but also views of himself. He is brought out of mental confinement to know and build himself by the other's !ooks, voices, and consciousness. Between Leventhal and others there exist, the conflicts of figurative looks, opinions, as well as those of literal looks. For example, Leventhal's opinions of Elena and her mother are disputed by Max.

The biggest conflict of opinions concerns Allbee's job loss; "the original scene in Rudiger's office" takes place between Allbee and Leventhal. Allbee insists that Leventhals rude speech and behaviour to Rudiger caused his loss of job, leading to his present miserable life. In addition he regards it as Leventhal's revenge for his anti-semitism. Allbee who imposes such opinion on Leventhal is a WASP, a member of the ruling class in the United States with the power to sway opinion and change perspectives, while Leventhal is a Jew, a member of a minority group. Allbee is also an antisemite. He shows his anti-semitic attitude towards Leventhal before getting fired and still shows it to him after; he affirms that Jews cannot understant Thoreau or Emerson and call Jews "The children of caliban" (P. 129). Their views are divided on many things other than the cause of Allbee's present predicament. Between Leventhal and the Willistons, a WASP couple there is also a conflict of slant" (103). They consider Leventhal responsible for Allbee's present plight. Although against doing so Leventhal points out the anti-semitism underlying their views and the distortion in Phoebe Williston's view of Allbee;

"She did not want the facts; she warded them off... she probably knew what he [Allbee] was like. Oh, of course she kenw,..." My dear lady", Leventhal, protested in thought, "I don't ask you to look at things my ways, but just to look. That would be enough. Have a look ! ... Believe me, he is not what Phoebe says". (1992-93).

The WASP's powers to sway opinion and to impose their realities on minority groups profoundly influence the minorities' self-images. Scared by a blacklist, society's ruling power, and being called "Caliban" (P. 129) by Allbee Leventhal points it out to the Willistons: "My God ! We (Jews) have a name for everything except what we really think and feel" (P. 103). However, it was Rudiger's low evaluation of him that caused Leventhal to lose his head.

"But why had he [Leventhal] lost it (his head) ? only because of Rudiger's abuse? No, he, he himself and begun to fear that the lowest price he put on himself was too high and he could scarcely understand why anyone should want to pay for his services. And under Rudiger's influence he had felt this. He made me believe what I was afraid of, Leventhal thought (P. 107). The self images imposed on Leventhal by the others, especially by WASPs, lead further to self-hatred, Leventhals' unreasonably low evaluation of Jews, which Harkavy calls "ghetto psyschology" (P. 116, 223), can be considered "Jewish self-hartred". [12] Why, you are succumbing yourself to all the things that are said against us Jews). (P. 116)

Elena's mother also hates the Jews and she does not accept her daughter's marriage with a Jew i.e. Max very easily. "She is a very peculiar type of person, my mother. She acted terrible when Max and I got married. She wanted to throw me out of the house because I was going with him. I couldn't bring him in I had to meet him outside".

''Max mentioned once or twice..." "She is an awfully strict catholic, she said if I married anybody but a catholic she wouldn't have any more to do with me. She would curse me. So when I left the house she did. 1 didn't even see her until Phillie was born. I still don't see he much, but since Mickey is sick she is here pretty often. If max is home, she wont't even come in. She is very superstitions, my mother has all the old-country ways". (P.52)

Elena's mother is so against the Jews that if anything happened to the boy she would consider it in the nature of a judgement on the marriage. The marriage was impure to her Yes, the understood how she felth about it. A Jew, a man of wrong blood, of bad blood, had given her daughter had given her daughter two children, and that was why this was happening. (P. 54)

The images of people in miserable plights, which appear in one of the two epigraphs of this novel, frequently come into Leventhal's mind:

"There rose immediately to Levethal's mind the most horrible images of men wearily sitting on mission benches waiting for their coffee in a smeared and bleary winter sun; of flophouse sheets and filthy pillows". (P. 61)

To tell the truth Leventhal leading a secure life now, has scrambled up from such a predicament and to use his won words, has "got away with it" (P. 16)

Allbe's present plight reminds him of the problem of destiny. Leventhal says to himself impatiently, "There are two billion people or so in the world and his is (Allbee) miserable what's he *so* special?" (P. 134) Micey's rare disease, the other main event in this novel, makes Leventhal conscious of the problem of destiny.

"It [Mickey's disease] was rare well, did medicine have any idea how a thing like that singled out a child in staten Island rather than say, st. Louis or Denver? One child in thousands. How did they account for it?" (P. 56)

Of the problem of destiny, Leventhal and Allbee also have different points of view. (P. 130) Albee puts forward a theory similar to (Calvinistic) determinism, saying that "people have a destiny forced on them" (P. 62), that "when it came to the important things in my life, I never had a chance to choose" (P. 172) and so on. He even says to Leventhal, who does not accept his deterministic thought (P. 62), that Jews have the theory of free will.

[Albee said] It doesn't enter your mind, does it- that a man might not be able to help being hammered down? If a man is down, a man like me, it's his fault .... It's a Jewish point of view. You will find it all over the Bible... we do get it in the neck for nothing

and suffer for nothing, and there's no denying evil
is as real as sunshine... to you the whole thing is
that I must deserve what 1 get.... You sure can't
understand what makes a man drink. (Leventhal
said), All right, so I can't". (P. 130)
Their views of destiny, of life, are also divided in this way.

As a ruling class WASP, Allbee flaunts his privileged
Puritan family birth by saying, "one of my ancestors was
Governer Winthrop. Governor Winthrop! and then by
calling Jews "The children of Caliban. (P. 129) The Puritans,
Congregational Protestants, who imigrated' to America in
the seventeenth century, held to the conviction that they the
could foresee God's predestination, and that they themselves
held this conviction to salvation, while Orthodox Puritans
did not have such a belief.[13] Albee illustrates that WASPs
justify their view and reinforce this justification by means
of the rhetoric that declares that they and their views are
warranted by God. Leventhal disputes Allbee's elitism in
his heart: "God was no respecter of persons, meaning that
there were the same rules for everybody. (P. 57) an allusion
to Colossians 3:25 and to "The world wasn't made for you
any more than it was for me". (P. 71)

We (WASPs) thought it would be daylight forever"
(P. 129) an ominous shadow, however has begun looming
over the WASP's privileged social city" (P. 64) in Allbee's
words, WASP power has begun to be menaced by the Jew's
rapid advance. In addition, Allbee himself has almost no
social power, the only ground left for his elitism and for the
validity of his views is the religions one.

"Well of course. 1 have lived in New York for a long time. It's a very Jewish city, and a person would have to be a pretty sloppy observer not to learn a lot about Jews here. You know yourself how many Jewish dishes there are in the cafeterias, how much of the state-how many Jewish comedians and jokes, and stores, and Jews in public life, and so on. You know that. It's no revelation". (P. 64)

Albee's and Leventhal's opinions are obviously in conflict with each other but whose view is true? Concerning Leventhal's view of Elena, Jonathon Baumbach writes that Bellow takes us to no discoverable final truth, only to a profound and ambiguous approximation of it. The truth is not unveiled because of the narrative structure of this novel. The extent of the narrators information is confined to that of Leventhal as a fixed internal localization. Therefore, there cannot be an objective judgement on, whose view is the right one.

Allbee has tried to validate his narrative as Leventhal's victim. However, with the disclosure of his inebriety, a probable cause of his discharge, he begins to abandon his narrative.

"I have to change... I must... get back to what I was when Flora was alive. I feel worthless. I know what I am. I am to blame. I know it". (P. 174-75)

He abandons his elitism, his ground for the superiority of WASPs, himself, and his views.

"When I was young I had my whole life laid out in my mind. I planned that it was going to be like on the assumption that I came out of the lords of the earth. I had all kinds of expectations. But God disposes. There's no use Kidding". (P. 208)

Later, after a long separation since his attempted suicide, Allbee meets Leventhal at a theatre by accident and says to him:

> "I have made my peace with things as they are... I am not the type that comes to terms with whoever runs things; what do I care" The world wasn't exactly made for me. What I am going to do about it? ... Approximately made for me will have to be good enough. All the stiffness of once upon a time, that's gone that's gone... Anyway I am enjoying life..."

"Wait a minute, what's your idea of who runs things ?" said Leventhal" (P. 264)

The passage shows at once that Albee makes his peace with "things as they are" or accepts or respects things as they are: "Things as they are" differentiates itself both from what Allbee thinks things are and from what other think things are. "Things as they are" must always be beyond human congnizance. They are the things (the world) seen from nobody's perspective, from God's standpoint that human beings cannot reach. To use Allbee's words cited just above, things are not made exactly for him.

> "You are a true Jew, Leventhal, You have the true horror of drink. We are the sons of Belial to you, we smell of whisky worse than of sulphur. When Noah lies drunk- you remember that story ? His gentile- minded sons have a laugh at the old man, but his Jewish son is horrified. There's truth in that story. It's a true story" (P. 67)

Allbee remarks about Leventhal. Asa is having complex in his mind, only because he is a Jew. But though being a son of a Jew-person, Philip, Asa's nephew does not know Jew language. And Allbee uses this small child to take revenge of Leventhal. That is a greatest example of Jew hatred of the WASPs.

"Ruf mir Yoshke, ruf mir Moshke"
"Aber gib Mir die groschke".

"Call me Ikey, call me Moe, but give me the dough. What's it to me if you despise me ? What do you think equality with you means to me? what do you have that I care about except the groschen?" That was his (Leventhal's) father's view. But not his. He rejected it and recoiled from it. Anyway, his father had lived poor and died poor, that stern proud old fool with his savage looks, to whom nothing mattered save his advantage and to be freed by money from the power of his enemies. And who were the enemies? The world, everyone. They were imaginary. There was no advantage. He carried on like a merchant prince among his bolts and remnants, and was willing to be a pack rat in order to become a lion. There was no advantage; he never became a lion. It gave Leventhal pain to think about his father's sense of these things"(P.99)

This passage is very important in the novel, because it reflects the difference of 'views' between Leventhal and his father. Leventhal does not want to bend before the W. A. S. Ps or any other persons due to his Jewishness, but wants to create a new culture. But his father is an oppressed one. He fears others and tells Asa also to do so.

But Asa has a revolutionary mind. He fights against the injustice done to him by Allbee. "If you believe I did it on purpose, to get even, then it's not only because I am terrible personally but because I am a Jew" (P. 103) Asa understands very well that only because he is a Jew, Allbee is troubling him. "That sounds fine, Stan. But it adds up to the same things, as far as I am concerned. You think that he burned me up and I wanted to get him in bad. Why? Because I am a Jew; Jews are touchy, and if you hurt them they won't forgive you. That's the pound of flesh. Oh, I know you think there isn't any room in you for that; I's a superstition. Every once in a while you will hear people say, "That's from the middle Ages". My God! we have a name for everything except what we really think and feel," (P. 103)

Asa knows that in American culture, Jews and their activities are given certain names. Their culture is not readily accepted by the W.A.S. Ps. Asa's staunch nature and revolt against the discrimination can be clearly seen from his following words. "What, wipe the spit off may face and leave like a gentlmen ? I wouldn't think much of myself if I did." (P. 105) The Jews in 'The Victim' are not orthodox. They are not stuck to their old traditions and customs.

"Whatever comes to hand, I think. Nowadys, theater reminiscences-he used to be a theatrical man. But science, too, I hear. You know, I can't read Yiddish." (P. 110) Harkavy being a Jew doesn't know Jewish language. But all the Jews are proud of their culture and their leaders. "The (Disraeli) showed Europe that a Jew could be a national leader" said Goldstone. "That's Leventhal all over for you", exclaimed Harkavy. That shows you where he stands". Jews and Empires? Suez and India and so on? It never seemed right to me.

"You being up Bismarck, "he said" why did he say Jude instead of Englishman? Disraeli was a bargainer, so he was a Jew to him; naturually".

'Don't misrepresent Bismarck on the Jew's, warned Harkavy. Be 'careful, boy; he lightened their load".

'Yes, he had something to say about making a great race. What was it, now? "A German stallion and a Jewish mare.

The Jews could discuss about their leaders & their contribution in a modern Jewish culture. They could even point out their faults.

"I don't have it in for him. But he wanted to lead England. In spite of the fact that he was Jew, not because he cared about empires so much. People laughed at his nose, so he took up boxing; they laughed at his (Disraeli) poetic silk clothes, so he put on black; and they laughed at his books, so he showed them. He got into politics and became the prime minister. He did it all on nerve." (P. 116).

A Jewish prime Minister also had to face hatred and pinching comments. The hatred for Jews is a part of W. A. S. Ps culture. Saul Bellow is successful in telling the worse condition of the Jews and their culture in America.

"Because you have got to blame me that's why, said Allbee. You won't assume that it isn't entirely my fault. It's necessary for you to believe that I deserve what I get. It doesn't enter your mind, does it-that a man might not be able to help being hammered down ? What do you say? Maybe he can't help himself? No, if a man is down, a man like me, it's

his fault. If he suffers, he's being punished. There
is no evil in life itself. And do you know what? It's
a Jewish point of view, you will find it all over the
Bible, God doesnt' make mistakes. He is the
department of weights and measures. If you are
okay, he is okay, too. That's what Job's friends come
and say to him. But 1 will tell you something. We
do get it in the neck for nothing and suffer for
nothing, there is no denying that evil is as real as
sunshine. Take it from me, I know what I am talking
about. To you the whole thing is that I must deserve
what I get. That leaves your hands clean and its
unnecessary for you to bother yourself. Not that I
am asking you to feel sorry for me, but you sure
can't understand what makes a man drink". (P. 130)

Allbee always points out Asa's Jewishness and compels
him to feel that whatever is happening with him is only
because he is a Jew. And for this same reason, Allbee
purposefully resides in Aas's house. And he take undue
advantage of Asa's sober nature Asa's nephew dies, but
even though the people around him are not ready to forget
Jewishness and Christiany. Elena, his mother undoubtedly
insists on a catholic funeral.

Some critics write that Leventhal's question ("What's
your idea who runs things?") which the Nazis were asked
on trial in Nuremburg (Miller 30), remains an insoluble
mystery because Albee does not answer. It is true that
readers cannot obtain Allbee's "idea of who runs things",
but at the same time, judging from his question, Leventhal

does not consider himself the person 'who runs things. In any case, Allbee abandons his elitism.

Leventhal, who thought "there was great unfairness in one man's having all the comforts of life while another had nothing" (P. 70-71) now changes his views.

"In Leventhal's mind, this (his success) was not even a true injustice, for how could you call anything so haphazard an injustice ? It was a shuffle, all, all accidental and haphazard [256].

It is clear from this passage that Leventhal now considers life so haphazard as to be out of human control. In other words, he clearly negates both the theories of free will and congregational determinism that Allbee has entertained. Furthermore, Leventhal thinks:

> "There was a wrong emphasis. A & though a man really could be made for say Burke-Beard and company... This was wrong. But the error rose out of something very mysterious, namely. A promise had been made. In thinking of this promise, Leventhal compared it to a ticket, a theater... why should tickets, mere tickets more be promised if promises are being made-tickets to desirable and undersirable places? There were more important things to be promised. Possibly there was a promise, since so many felt it. He himself was almost ready to affirm that there was. But it (a promise) as misunderstood. (P. 256-57)

His doubt of such promises is that of theological determinism. In any case, it is not to be denied that he thinks a promise in other words, "truth" (P. 77,151)', is beyond human congnizance. It does lead to a negation of American Puritanism, which considers God's predestination within human congnizance. It also follows that life is beyond human understanding, which tends to place it between "desirable" or undersirable"! Leventhal also comes to respect "things as they are", the world beyond human congnizance.

Leventhal, however, does not learn this acceptance completely on his own. Harkavy, Schlossberg and Mary advise Leventhal to accept "things as they are". Harkavy advises Leventhal who is so excessively swayed by the other's opinions as to feel Jewishness self hatred, to accept himself as he is:

> "If you don't mind, Asa, there is one thing I have to point out that you have learned... you want the whole world to like you... Why isn't it enough for you that some do ? Why can't you accept the fact that others never will? .... Too bad people., don't know what I am really like ... All I can say is... we all have our faults and we are what we are I have to take myself as I am or push off (die). I am all I have in the world. And with all my shortcomings my life is precious to me... a little independence, boy". (P. 7 8)

Why you are succumbing yourself to all the things that are said against us (Jews) (P. 116).

Schlossberg's and Mary's advice are similar to Harkavy's Schlossberg, who agrees neither with realistic Benjamin making a Mock of Judeo Christian messianism nor with idealistic Harkavy, advises Leventhal to accept, "things at they are", saying, "It's bad to be less than human and it's bad to be more than human. P. 119) Many, as Leventhal remembers disregards anti-Semitism and advises him to be sure of himself.

Respecting "things as they are" is characteristic of both Allbee's change and Levanthal's probably something he (Leventhal) had no right to resist". (P. 141) Mickey's rare disease is one of the "things as they are". "Things as they are" can be God's dispensation nobody is privileged to know, because they both invoke God.[14] In any case, "things as they are" cannot be identical with what I think things are or with what others think things are. Thy cannot be the world seen from anybody's perspective. It is the world seen from nobody's perspective, nobody's word. Nobody's world, which always escapes human cognizance, can be a solution of the dilemma of Asa.

"Nobody's world" ("things as they are") brings about the solutions to the various problems in the novel: the groundlessness of anti - Semitism and WASP ish elitism; the meaninglessness of interpreting lives as fortunte or unfortunate; the relativity of human views; the respect of the world beyond human cognizance; Jewish self- discovery in America. In respect to the problem of responsibility that some critics consider to be the main theme of this novel, it neccessarily follows that human beings are not completely responsible for what they do because things are beyond the sway of their free will. And in respect to the problem of the Victim, the title of this fiction which never appears in the text- it follows that the dichotomy of assailant and victim can easily be subverted and can even become almost meaningless.

Both Allbee and Leventhal exchanging their perspectives and voices (consciousnesses) with the other, come to consider nobody's world ("things as they are"), which human cognition (perspective) or narratives in general cannot reach as the ultimate standard or truth. The victim is a narrative in which the characters come to accept the world without any narrative or any interpretation. To put it another way, The victim is a narrative negating the fundamental truth of narrative in general because they must be narrated from someone's perspective.

Character's looks (perspectives) voices, and consciousness as has been pointed out, are mixed with one another. What then is the relationship between the characters (the protagonist) and the narrater (the author) ? In this fiction identifying the narrator is a big problem. Because the narrator's information as mentioned earlier, is confined to that of Leventhal's, it follows that only Leventhal's thoughts are narrated. It is almost impossible to distinguish between Leventhal's thoughts, presented by means of free indirect thought, and the narrator's narration (especially telling), because they have the same grammatical structure in a third-person narrative. It does not seem unnatural for all the third person pronouns to be changed into Leventhal.

The narrator's perspectives and voice are mixed with Leventhal's. The Victim results from the mixture, from dual ('double") perspective and voice. There are many reasons to confirm this conclusion. Roy Pascal writes of Saul Bellow as a contemporary writer who powerfully continues the tradition of free indirect discourse.[15] which is the characteristic of the change of narrative mode from "Dangling man" to "The Victim". The narrative world of "The Victim" is not an objective world, for the prrotagonist's thoughts are presented there. It is nobody's world prresented by means of free indirect discourse mode, the mixture of the narrator's and the protagonists discourses. The Victim can be a narrrative negating narratives in general, for the characters come to see that they cannot reach nobody's world ("things as they are"). Yet the truth is that the narrative world is "things as they are" resulting from nobody's perspectives.

The Victim reflects the modern Jewish culture, where all the characters try to create a new culture but the WASPs or the anti-Jewish people don't allow to do them so. Asa is fighting very hard to create his own existence, but proves to be unsuccessful. The charge which Allbee puts on Asa seems fantastic when he hears it. But it is significant that Saul Bellow persistently reminds us of Leventhal's gnawing sense of guilt. And he is finally, though grudgingly, forced to assume responsibility. He asks, "I haven't thought about you in years; frankly, and I don't know why you think I care whether you exist or not what, are we related?" "By blood? No.. Heavens" (P. 29) answers Allbee. The theme is thus explicitly stated: how man is related to man, not by blood, of Jew to Jew but as man caught in the tangled web of social reality. The force of the conviction however does not rest so much on the 'apparent' justice of Allbee's complaint as in the convert intimidations with which he often frequents Leventhal's house appealing for sympathy and gradually Leventhal gives him almost everything he asks; for money to tide over his difficulties and bed in his apartment. Allbee consciously reminds him of the fate which Leventhal secretly believes is his, insistently identifying Leventhal "a deep Hebrew" with the racial characteristics of "his people", implying thereby that Jew is outside the human community, a community to which this degraded, drifting alcoholic, a gentile really belongs.

In the Jewish culture in "The Victim", the paradox of anti-semitism in which the Jew is forced to be more than others and is actually accused of betraying human values precisely by those who are inhumanly treating him is thus articulated. The novel exposes the Jew's own sense of guilt for Leventhal is both the victim and the victimizer.

Leventhal's association with Allbee confirms his awareness of the limitation that humanity imposes. As the Talmud asserts "all Jews are mutually accountable to each other" and Leventhal "liked to think human accountable" In his moments of sobriety he is aware of his indifference, his own uneasy sense of possible guilt, as he feels himself deficient in virtue." People has a destiny forced on them and that's all the destiny they get" (P. 71) Allbee believe that man can change if he is willing to accept the immediacy of life. "Repent means now", he tells Leventhal "this minute and 'forever without wasting any more time" (P. 227)

Leventhal realizes his own limitations of the self and his obligations to the rest of the world. Although he initially repudiates his responsibility he gradually admits the ambiguous nature of his guilt seeing in Allbee an example of misery and desperation greater than his own. It is also significant that Leventhal's growing insight into the problem is provoked by the responsibilities imposed on him by his brother's family, besides Allbee. Again, Allbee's conviction that he has somehow been cheated of his rightful inheritance, his distinctive identity, is essentially one stemming from his sense of humanity and is not exclusively Jewish in its overtones.

A contrasting vision of life is offered by Schlossberg." the spokesman of reality". A writer of "whatever comes to hand" Schlossberg points out the futility of a vague aspiration for limitless life by under-lining man's morality. For him man's humanity lies neither in impatiently demanding perfection which he calls being more than human nor in responding to life without feeling, less than human. He clinches the issue by affirming. "It is bad to be less than human and it's bad to be more than human" (P. 133) This naturally leads him to an existential situation, an acceptance of the inevitability of death.

"There is limit to me. 1 have to be myself in full. Which is somebody who dies, isn't it? That's what I was from the beginning. I am not three people, four people, I was born once and I will die once. You want to be two people? More than human? May be its' because you don't know how to be one" (P. 255)

To be human, therefore, is to accept the responsibility of guilt and death that are the human conditions without hating oneself or others and this is the Jew's distinctive mode of acceptance, the life suffering implicit in this traditional culture. This awareness permits the Jew to experience life's corresponding greatness and beauty, equally real with Allbee's somber vision: "Choose dignity", he advises Leventhal, "Nobody knows enough to turn it down." (P. 134)

Scholossberg's philosophy justifies Leventhal's hope that despite the restraint of mortality, man can't go in all directions without any limit. Leventhal comes to realize that all men are somehow related and therefore in some way responsible accountable - as his own relationship with Allbee demonstrates.

Leventhal, however, seems unwilling to accept his won responsibility as an integral part of his destiny as a human being. This becomes obvious from his last chance meeting with Allbee in a theatre where Allbee admits that he has capitulated to "who ever runs things". Allbee's reconciliation is the result of surrendering his vestigial sense of self to survive in a world he has made for himself. Nevertheless, Levethal demands, still intent on knowing' "what is your idea of who run things". (P.294) But Allbee has already disappeared, his encounter being a painful reminder to Leventhal that if he cannot choose reality, neither can he discount the possibility that somehow a choice exists. The irony is that Allbee has made "his peace" with the real world but with "his own paranoic vision of it" Leventhal, however, is groping in the dark, baffled as he is, with the problem of choice despite the infinite possibilities open to him.

Thus the development of Bellow's hero is from alienation to accommodation, from denial to acceptance. This accommodation as Marcus Klein has averred "has meant in all cases an impossible reconciliation, a learning to live with, and at the same time a learning to deny, what has been plainly there".[16] The Bellow hero confronts a strong sense of self, the sacrifice of self demanded by social circumstances and finally learns to humble himself in the intricate texture of reality. As Ihab Hassan has observed if "they (Bellows heroes) ends with humility they begin in humiliation." [17]

Notes:

1. Jonathan Baumbach," The Landscape of Nightmare" (New York 1965) p. 2.
2. Allen Tate, "Techniques of Fiction", The Man of Letters in the Modern world. (New York, 1955), P. 83.
3. Marius Bewley, "The Question of Form", The Eccentric Design (London 1959) P. 18
4. Ibid p. 18
5. Richard Chase", The Broken Circuit", The American Novel and it's Tradition (New York, 1957). P. 11
6. Norman Mailer, "Some Children of the Goddeess", Esquire, 60 (July 1963), p. 69.
7. Ihab Hassan, Saul Bellow: Five Faces of a Hero, Critique Vol. Ill (New York, 1966), p. 28.
8. Keith Michael Opdahl," The Novels of Saul Bellow: An Introduction" (The Pennsylvania State Unviersity, 1967) p.6.
9. Ibid, p.5.
10. Ibid, p. 27.
11. The relation of private capital to the Nazi regime has received many different interpretations. The story of I.G. Farben (I.G. = interessen gemeinschaft) has been told several times. The account by Joseph Borkin is Clear and readable. Peter Hayes provides a list of American and other accounts, including two works published like "The Victim" in 1947 (in New York) Howard Ambruster, "Treason's Peace" and Richard Sasuly, I.G. Farben. Farben's directors

were tried at Nuremburg, though their sentences were comparatively light.

12. Jewish self-hatred has been discussed since Theodor Lessing's Der Judische Selbsthaf (1930).

13. Morgan (34-35).

14. This is one of Leventhal's invocations of God: "God will help me out" passed through his (Leventhal's) mind, and he did not stop to ask himself exactly what he meant by this (P, 205)

15. Roy Pascal did not discuss Bellow's novels. He briefly referred to Bellow after discussing nineteenth - century European novels, It is worth mentioning that Pascal is one of Mikhail Bakhtin's elder brother's friends (Clark and Holquist 19).

16. Marcus Klein, "Saul Bellow: A Discipline of Nobility", After Alienation (New York, 1965), P. 33.

17. Ihab Hassan, "Saul Bellow", Radical Innocence (Princeton Unviersity Press, 1961), P. 291.

Chapter - III

LOCATION OF CULTURE IN ISAAC BASHEVIS SINGER'S SHOSHA

A) About the Author, Isaac Bashevis Singer:-

Singer's impassioned narrative art which roots in a Polish - Jewish cultural tradition, brings Universal human conditions to life[1]

He was born in Poland in 1904. Both his father and grandfather were rabbis and influenced him to a very great degree. While young, he received a basic Jewish education that eventually prepared him to follow his father's and grandfather's footsteps into the rabbinical vocation. The study of the Torah, the Talmud, the Cabala and other sacred Jewish books thus formed the basis of earlier thinking. The chief influence that transformed Singer from a rabbi into a writer, was that of his elder brother, the novelist I. J. Singer, who broke with the orthodoxy of his family and started writing secular stories. Singer was fascinated both by his parent's mysticism and his brother's rationalism.

After emigrating to the United States in 1935, Singer started working as a regular journalist and columnist for the New York Paper, the Jewish Daily, 'Forward'. Some of his early works were published in Warsaw; but nearly all his fiction has been written in Yiddish for his journal. It is only recently that Singer's work has been translated on any scale and that his merit as a Jewish novelist and as a modern novelist who uses traditional modes with incomparable skill, have been recognized by a general audience.

His publications include "A Friend of Kafka, The Slave, The Seance and other Stories, The Manor, The Estate, The Magician of Lublin, In my 'Fathers court' A crown of feathers and other stories, Enemies: A love story Shosha and Passions and other stories." His latest work published in 1988 is "The Death of Methuselah and other Stories".

Singer does not see himself as a fiction writer only; he is a recorder of Jewish history which he presents within the literary framework of the novel and the short story. As he says:

I hope that when people a hundred years from now
ask 'what happened to the Polish Jews in the
twentieth century that is now so far away. Someone
will answer-if you read Isaac Singer you may find
some clue'[2]

Singer has successfully presented the East European Yiddish tradition in a narrative style which is detached yet intimate.

Singer I. B., Shosha, New York Farrar Straus and Giroux, 1978. All subsequeni references to the text are from this edition.

He is now widely proclaimed as writer of Yiddish Literature standing clearly outside the mainstream and basic traditions of both Yiddish and American Literature.

In Singer on finds a rare combination of an old-fashioned story teller and a modern psychological writer. While Singer has been labelled for contemporary fiction, he has also been indicated for his obsession with the past and for his preferential treatment to a dying language like Yiddish in which he wrote almost all his novels. He has further been accused of setting his fiction in a world that hardly exists now. And yet he always succeeds in attracting modern readers chiefly because he believes that the only role of fiction is entertainment. In an interview given to Katha Politt, a poet and critic living in New York, Singer says.

Entertainment is a minimum and a must... only bad stories have to lean on the crutches of messages.[3]

Singer, thus, is confident of the requirement of entertainment value in his stories. A deep and clear observation of human nature and it's complexities and intricacies makes his writings absorbing and interesting. He not only writes with confidence he also has great faith in the intellectual receptivity of his readers

Singer's personal experiences are avowedly the basis of his work. "Most of what I learn now comes from life, not literature".[4] He has a strong conviction as writer that real characters come from real people, and real people have roots. He firmly believes that one cannot write a good novel about just A human Being; one has to pick a specific man or woman - a person 'with an address'. This adherence to experience and to traditional form do not, in any sense make Singer's novels uninteresting. As Malcolm Bradbury points out.

> Each new novel seems to arise from a creative
> curiosity generated by aback - and - forth motion
> between the detailing and analysis of an observed
> external world or a realm of knowable experience,
> and an inner working process that gives formal
> consistency; thus each novel creates its own world
> a fresh...[5] (Malcolm Bradbury "Possibilities")

Though Singer does not deliberately convey a message in his novels, the reader deciphers the belief that forms the basis of his novels. The fact that culture always remains, tradition never perishes, that transformation does not nearly transform but adds something to tradition, emerges as the logical conclusion of the thematic development of the novels. The novels are of course, rooted in a historical period, have historically authentic characters but they are not in any sense, dated. Singer's narrative virtuosity achieves the blurring of geographical and historical demarcations which characterize all great literature.

B) Isaac Bashevis Singer and the classical Yiddish Tradition:-

Isaac Bashevis Singer may well be the most widely ready Yiddish author of all time. Yet the popularity of his works in translation is not paralleled in the original among readers of Yiddish. While most of Singer's works appeared first in the Yiddish press (the novels serialized in the manner generally nineteenth century), only a few can be bought in the original language. Lest this be attributed solely to the general indisputable decline in the audience for Yiddish writing, it may be pointed out that a recent catalogue which lists three titles by the prolific Singer offers no fewer than nine by Sholem Asch and even by Singer's older brother Isarel Joshua. It is in fact disconcerting to discover with what vehemence many intelligent and experienced Yiddish readers reject the works of Singer, branding them not only as "worthless" but as "Pornographic" and even "degenerate". Evident in these evaluations to be sure, is the anxiety of many Jews to conceal from alien eyes the unflattering aspects of East European Jewish life which Singer so frequently depicts. Today, moreover, this concern represents more than simply the traditional resolve to avoid exposing to anti-semites Jewish shetl life at its most vulnerable. It reflects as well the urgent and pious desire to protect from misinterpretation the vanished east European culture of which Yiddish literature is the product; a culture which, because of its catastrophic demise, is understandably surrounded with an elegiac aura.

Study of Yiddish literature, however, reveals that the classical Yiddish literary 'tradition itself is not predominantly one of prettification; that the sores and boils which afflicted East European Jewish life were plainly evident to the older writers and were unabashedly treated in their literary works. The observation that Isaac Bashevis Singer frequently presents Jews in "a bad light" is certainly accurate. But the same accusation could be made against I. L. Peretz, Sholem Asch, I. J. Signer, certainly Mendele Moykher Sforim Aleichem. Nevertheless, however vaguely they perceive this, Singer does in fact represent a significant deviation from the tradition of Yiddish literature which more Yiddish readers accept and into which they expect modern Yiddish works to fit.

In lamenting his enforce exile from Germany and his consequent loss of contact with the German public, Thomas Mann once described his books as the product of a reciprocal educational bond between nation and author, depending on shared assumptions which the author himself had helped to create. Such a description can nowhere more accurately be applied than to the works of the older generation of Yiddish writes. Mendele Moykher Sforim, Sholem Aleichem and I. L. Peretz, the triad' of "classical" 'Yiddish writes, display considerable and significant difference from one another with respect to theme, style, and literary attitude. But they were all in the first instance social writers. That is to say, they viewed their writing directly in the context of the audience for whom they wrote. Mendele describes the inner struggle which preceded his division to brave struggle which preceded his division to brave ridicule by writing in the despised Yiddish tongue, instead of in the Hebrew as previously. The struggle was resolved when he asked himself, "For whom am I working?" And the answer came in this form: "Let come what will; I will take pity on the Yiddish language that outcast daughter. It is time to do something for the people" Sholem Aleichem refers to himself repeatedly as a folksshrayber, a writer of (for) the people, while one of Peretz's little known criticisms of Sholem Aleichem rests on the view that the latter" doesn't do things, doesn't call on people to do things do things, he makes us laugh".

This does not mean that classical Yiddish literature was necessarily programmatic. Mendele's work is openly tendentious, at first frankly preaching the message of enlightenment, a message whose inadequacy to the problem was progressively illuminated, even to the author himself, by the very fidelity and life of his era. Neither Peretz nor Sholem Aleichem promotes a particular program in his writing, yet their works, with all of the patent differences between them, share certain characteristics which are also to be found in those of Mendele. Central to the similarity is the view that the shtetl life of nineteenth century east European Jewry needed to be changed drastically, and the conviction that reform and progress were not only essential, but also possible. Mendele is unsparing in his castigation of Jewish civic leaders for their greed, ignorance, and complacency. Peretz writes scathingly of "dead towns' and Sholem Aleichem "begs the reader not to be offended that he speaks such harsh words to his Kasrilevke people. I am, you understand, my dear friends myself a Kasrileviker". Common to all three writers, and of greater importance than the element of social criticism which is evident in these examples is the assumption that the writer's function included the obligation to reproach, admonish, cajole and encourage his readers'. And this' assumption was shared by the readers who valued "their" writers partly in proportion to their efficacy as teachers.

Nevertheless, with the exception of Mendel, the prevailing 'tone of classical Yiddish literature' is not didactic. And even in the case of Mendele the author speaks as a member of the community from within the community to the membership as a whole, and thus feels free to criticize and attack without reservation regarding its weakness and evils, It is the sense of community which is pervasive in the older Yiddish literary tradition. This has hardly escaped notice.

However the frequent translation of this sense into the vague sensation of "warmth" which has come to be associated with Yiddish literature and particularly with the works of Sholem Aleichem rests upon the mistaken conclusion that the authors were describing a community actually achieved, rather than voicing their fervent aspirations toward community. All of the classicists in their different ways were concerned with the vast discrepancies between the community which ought to have been fostered by the practices which are virtually built into the traditional Jewish ethic-and what was the actual state of affairs. While the victimization of the shtetl Jews by the Czarist government is clearly potrayed, as well as their pauperization by economic forces beyond for those among the Jews who prey on other Jews or who are indifferent to their sufferings. There is sufficient evidence to suggest that the older writers viewed social injstice within the Jewish shtetl as a prevailing rather than an exceptional evil. Despite this, they are never tempted to question the validity of the nation of Jewish community, with all the sympathy that they demonstrate towards the most down trodden among the Jews, and their anger at the Jewish oppressors, they rarely approach class consciousness.

Without doubt there existed within the shtetl alongside of the social divisions and inequities, genuinely community solidarity which crossed class lines. The concept of Jewish religion being the privilege of a chosen people whose distinctiveness was continually emphasized by their residence among an alien majority, made religious belief and practice virtually conterminous with internal solidarity. The very notion of the Knesses Yisroel was part of the sacred component of Jewish life. Not only did the many ritual practices and traditionally prescribed attitudes contribute to social cohesion within the shtetl, but no less importantly, the existence of the east European Jewish community as an enclave within a generally hostile environment. While the very rich could escape most of the disabilities of Jewishness in the pale, in the typical shtetl rich and poor shared at the very least the fear of pogroms. In spite of considerable ugly historical evidence of actions enlisting the aid of the government to defect or suppress their rivals within the Jewish community, community solidarity was, at least in theory, viewed as necessary to protection and even survival, especially in times of increased pressures from without. For the classical Yiddish writers therefore, and for much although for no means' all of their readership the integrity of the shtetl community was an axiomatic norm representing an ideal type, in spite of the serious deviations from it in practice.

It is not clear that to what extent the classicists actually believed that their visions of Jewish community would be achieved. There is nevertheless implicit in traditional Yiddish literature the rationalist conviction that improvement was possible, that social controls could be imposed, and that the forces of cohesion could be 'made' to prevail. These forces were regarded as fundamental, no matter how weak they had became, while the shocking conditions which the writers angrily exposed, even if predominant, were viewed as symptoms and consequences of the aberrant breakdown of social order. The founders were not only rationalists, but also, whatever their personal religious conventions, essentially secular writers. Their central literary concentration was upon "the Jewish question" and this meant for them, without exception, the question of the Jew in the modern world. None of them conceived of a Jewish solution in any sort of withdrawer from the world. As secular writers, to be sure, they reflected the concerns of only a segment's of the Yiddish speaking population. Chassidim, for example, did not read Yiddish literature on principle for worldly literature was to them at worst trey and at best trivial. Other segments of the population, particularly some varieties of Zionists, rejected Yiddish literature not for its secular orientation but for its use of the despised Yiddish "Zhargon" a literary vehicle. Nevertheless, a broad range of readers coming largely from the working and middle classes was secured. And the equally fervent commitment of the founders to communal integrity and to social justice made it possible for readers at every point of a spectrum ranging from class conscious workers to comfortable petit - commercants to find in traditional Yiddish literature their cultured sustenance and an echo of their own shtetl experiences.

The shtetl of Isaac bashevis Singer is at once both reminiscent of and strangely different from that of the Yiddish classicists. It has often been remarked that the body of traditional Yiddish literature offers so clear and detailed a picture of shtetl culture that it can serve virtually as a source of ethnographic data. To the insider, the reader who himself emerged from it, it is instantly recognizable. The outsider, on the other hand, requires elaborate explanations, or at least a glossary, to orient himself in the environment Singer's shtetl presents largely the same landmarks. Yet it is unacknowledged by most remaining shtetl emigrants, while readers from "outside" appear to find their way about easily. Neither the motivations of Singer's characters nor their destinies are dependent on the specific cultural content of shtetl existence. His primary concern is with the perpetual struggle between good and evil for the soul of man; a struggle while goes on constantly, and primarily on a plane of human existence which has little to do with the rational. The physical as well as the cultural environment are important only as a viewing device through which this immanent struggle becomes manifest in dimensions which are temporally and spatially definable. The shtetl of the classicists is primarily comprehensible in terms of the social community which its represents or aspires to become. The shtetl of Singer is not a community at all. It is a society in disarray, Singer's which he sees as endemic to the condition of the world.

In Family Moskat, The Slave and Satan in Goray the absence of stable social relations and effective social controls is literal and is historically conditioned. With some exceptions such a situation is implicit in most of Singer's work. This vision, however, is not primarily a comment on society, Singer is not in the first instance concerned with the pernicious effect of the dissolution of social bonds although this is surely part of his theme in Satan in Goray. Rather, it permits the author virtually to ignore any distracting social context and allows him to present the actions and motivations of his people in "pure" almost abstract light, unencumberd by the complications which would be entailed in placing them in a culturally delimited delimited network of social relations. The shtetl which, incidently, Singer does not describe in very great detail, thus serves him as a kind of stylized exotic backdrop before with pious Jews and demons can play out their roles with equal appropriateness. The fact that humans and devils appear equally real in Singers' shtetl suggests that his Zionism, all of which can be located histrocially and geographically, are more products of the imagination than the invented Tuneyadevke and Glupsk of Mendel, or Sholem Aic chem's Kasri levke and Kozodeyevke.

Singer's modernism as a Yiddish author consists in the fact that his concern is not primarily with the "Jewish question" but rather with the human condition; and moreover that those aspects of humanity which are to him most fascinating are the nonrationaL His style is vividly realistic and this makes even more striking the impression, objectionable to many traditional Yiddish readers, that to the author a succubus and a Yeshiva literature did not exclude the occult. Faithful recorders record many elements of folk belief in their works: blessings, curses, spirits, charms to ward off the evil, and the like. But these were always identified as superstition, as symptoms of backwardness, and were treated with ridicule or condescension. Mendele viewed them with the scornful laughter of the enlightened "Modernist". Sholem Aleichem with the indulgent amusement of a grandchild enjoying his grandmother's archaic antics. Peretz deliberately employed folk beliefs as literary devices and thus spared them his scorn. But as can be seen in his chassidic tales, he employed them for consciously rationalistic possibilities rather than with their significance to the nonrational component of human existence. The intensely traditionalist classidic milieu from which Singer came saw no sharp separation between the natural and the supernatural, nor, for the matter, between the religious and the matter, between the religious and the magical. Singer's chassidic shtetl (and we may stretch the term here to include the Warsaw of this childhood) is central to his writing not as a matrix for social relations but as an arsenal of characters, motifs, legends, and incidents all having equal claim to reality as material for his writing. In Singer's literary shtetl however, one distinction that was crucial to the chassidic view appears to grow dim- the distinction between the sacred and the profane. If, as Emile Durkheim maintained, that which is sacred in any society stands in part for the society itself in the collective representations of its members, then the encroachment of the profane in Singer's shtetl becomes a metaphor for the asocial environment in which his stories occur.

Much has been made in the Yiddish criticism of Singer's writing of his alleged pornography. The accusation requires no refutation but its relevance to the acceptance of Singer's work by Yiddish readers is not without interest. Themes such as aberration are not new to Yiddish literature, going back as for as Sholem Aleichem ("The man from Buenos Aires", "A Daughter's Grave"), and recurring frequently, for example 'in the works of Sholem Asch and David' Bergelson, both of whom are unhesitatingly admitted to the Yiddish cannon. New is Singer is his attention to sexuality of both men and women as a serious motivating force in human conduct, and of course, his fashionably frank description of sexual behaviour, as well as other orders of physiological function. It might be noted that most of Singer's stories appeared first in the Jewish daily "Forward". This had made it easy for some critics to accuse him of exploiting sectionalism to please the "lower" tastes of Forward readers- a charge which has been levelled in general against the forward since the days of Abraham Cahan. The readers of Yiddish belles letters are an old- fashioned group, although not more so than their years entitle them to be . Moreover, they are for the most part readers who cultivated formal education, either through their individual efforts or in groups related to trade unions, political organizations, or other voluntary associations interested in culture. To many of them, as is not uncommon with cultural noveaux arrives, culture is inseparable from gentility and the Yiddish genteel tradition rejects the sexual and physiological vulgarity, which critics tend to explain in commercial terms.

Much more important with regard to his reception, however, is the fact that Singer, writing in Yiddish, does not write primarily as a Jewish writer in the sense in which Yiddish readers view the terms. The destruction of the Yiddish speaking heartland and of its population in the early 1904's truncated the development of the Yiddish literary tradition at the point which it had reached in 1939. It also turned the attention of the Yiddish reader even further back, to fix for all time as typical of the vanished east European Jewish culture an idealized earlier shtetl which had in any case by that time ceased to exist. Since the 1940's Yiddish literature has to a considerable extent been concerned with the mineralization of this lost world of east European Jewry. For a number of individual writers, survivors of ghettos, death camps, and partisan groups, their writing is a personal act of piety. This is seen as the appropriate concern of Yiddish literature by large numbers of readers who themselves betray an acute awareness that they too are last survivors of a culture catastrophically destroyed, although of such as judgment. Singer, who in Satan in Goray had already indicated the direction in which he was to proceed, continued along the path of modernism as part of the development of world literature in the forties, fifties and sixties. His treatment of the human existential problem appears to Yiddish readers incomprehensibly aloof from the real, historical existential crisis which they experienced in their own lifetime. Whatever historic or sentimental bonds Singer, the man and the Jew shares with the Yiddish reading public, the gulf between his literary premises and their expectations is vast. The assumptions shared by the classical Yiddish writer and their readers gave great moral relevance to their works within the Jewish community. The fact that Singer, using the same props, as it were, communicates primarily with a public to 'whom the shtetl is essentially alien, suggests to these readers that his work is somehow spurious.

The readers of classical Yiddish literature were conditioned to find in their reading indications of a rational world of progress, hope, and brotherly assistance, and the unmistakable assurance of the author's adherence to these values. Singer describes instead an irrational, asocial universe, where as often as not as one writer has said, the devil has the last word. Unable to reconcile his shtetl with "their own" shtetl as potrayed, for example, by Sholem Aleichem, it is perhaps not surprising bewilderment as to which side Singer is really on.

C) **Outline of Shosha:**

Shosha is involved in several women whose originals appear in Singer's memories. Aaron is living with Dora and even while living with her he gets involved with Haiml's wife, Celia and shortly thereafter with Betty Slonim, the mistress of an American millionaire and then with Tekla, a Polish maid. In this aimless love - life, Aaron often remembers his childhood sweetheart Shosha.

Aaron Greidinger, the protagonist of "Shosha" is a playwright chasing wisdom and girls in Warsaw. He has grown up in Poland between the world wars amid the chaos caused by Russian Revolution. But the trauma that he has to bear is the separation from his childhood sweetheart, 'Shosha' a person mentally and physically retarded. Shosha is the story of this young writer's obsessive devotion; with all his hedonistic pursuits to Shosha. Apart from Aaron other characters are equally interesting in Shosha. Dr. Feitelzon for instance, an earthy mystic, San Drieman, the American construction millionaire, trying all the time to promote his mistress, the actress Betty Solmin. Then there are female characters who seem to fall over one another in their love for young Aaron. Celia Chentshiner is a hot-blooded ex-Hasid in her thirties who explains to Aaron that she likes gentleness, but not in bed. She is a melancholy woman. Her enlightened; and homosexual husband invites Aaron to share his wife's bed - Dora, a communist with prodigious breasts lectures the young writer on his failing capitalist degeneracy and rolls in bed with him humorously and reports later that she had indulged in some foreplay, some during play and even some after play. Tekla, the fair haired gentile Polish peasant maid, a devoted rustic cleans Aaron's flat and serves him in every way. Aaron sets off on a fling with her. Betty Slomin is a lovely actress from America for whom Aaron is commissioned to write a play. The play fails, but not before Araon seduces its leading lady.

Committed to literary career but not happy with his achievements Aaron astonishingly executes a great leap backward by marrying his childhood sweetheart Shosha while on a sight seeing tour with Betty Solmin, Aaron meets Shosha and is surprised to find that she has neither grown not aged during the last twenty years. His friends ask him as to what he has seen in the physically and mentally retarded girl Shosha Aaron answers. 'I see myself. Even now Shosha wears pigtails, eats candy, and has never been with a man. Aaron refers to Shosha as a child but also as a chaste Jewish daughter almost like his mother when she was a girl. What Aron sees in Shosha is not only his own lost innocence but a vanished way of life. When Aaron's mother, sister and brother returns to Krochmalna street for his wedding, they marvel at the changelessness of the street. Shosha too remains unchanged in contrast to Aaron's total transformation. Lawrence Friedman comments that "it is a timeless world of their Jewishness that Araon sporadically yearns to return, but of course, cannot."

Betty Slomin's offer of a convenient marriage and a visa with the financial blessings of Dreiman is turned down by Aaron. Rejecting the Visa to America offered by Dreiman, he chooses to live with Shosha, on the Krochmalana street where they grew up, and awaits the ruin that impends for them all Aaron's obsessive attachment to Shosha and his marriage with her is commented upon her by Leon Wiesettier. "Their union is mad", writes wiesettier, "but it is Griedinger's sole avenue through despair, his only triumph. And Singer's as well; implausible Shosha in the genuinely affecting image of an immobility as delusive as it is fearless.

Edward Alexander in his analysis of Shosha, comments that "the recrudescence of death in life, and the ambigious relation between the living and the dead obsess many of the characters in Shosha. Betty says to Aaron that "the past generations are our dybbuks... A person is literally a cemetery where multitudes of living corpses are buried. Haiml asks: "How can it be all the generations are dead and only we schlemiels are allegedly living?" Shosha is a creature of the past. When she and Aaron flee to escape the Germans she suddenly "sat down" on the road and "a minute later she was dead... Like mother Rachel".

Aaron shares with other Singer's heroes the incapacity to return to real Jewishness. Aaron's pursuit for pleasure or his flight from religion can succeed, the former because it grows by what it feeds on the latter because "we are running away and Mount Sinai after us. This chase has made us sick and mad". Alan Lelechuk comments that the hero does not get sick and mad though he has bouts of sickness and madness - as perhaps, his temperament and circumstances dictate. Instead the author permits him exit quietly from Poland and eventually, take up life anew in America, while an external madness (Nazism) has obliterated the other characters.

Haiml Chentshiner and intellectuals like Aaron's literary Mentor Morris Feit Elzohn who could flee, remain in Poland deliberately yielding to the future. For Aaron and the rest, sex provides the release from time. Sex is again the ultimate goal of Feltelzoh's spiritual expenditions and obsessively in Shosha than in Singer's other novels. Today's Jews like three things- Sex, Torah and Revolution, all mixed together. Give them those and they will raise to the skies.

In Shosha there is that mix of all three. The Jew's obsessive longing for Messaih Aaron. He says if you give a Jew one Messaih, he asks for another. Implicit in their longing is probably the enternal quest for answer to the questions regarding meaning and purpose of human life, is always given up by Singer's protagonists. The ambiguities remain unresolved.

Preservation of old Jewish values has always been one of the major themes of Singerian fiction. Shosha and her mother still observe the faith and carry on the ancient traditions. It is this innocence that makes Aaron to forsake his chance to marry Betty and leave for America before the Nazi invasion. In the realist setting of this novel, Singer shows a sensitive, thoughtful individual caught between contending drives.

D) Location of culture in Shosha:

In Shosha, the first chapter opens with the lines, "I was brought up on three dead languages - Heberw, Aramaic and Yiddish (some consider the last not a language at all) - and in a culture that developed in Babylon: the Talmud. The Cheder where I studied was a room in which the teacher ate and slept, and his wife cooked. There I studied not arithmetic, geography physics, chemistry, or history, but the laws governing an egg laid on a holiday and sacrifices in a temple destroyed two thousand years ago. Although my ancestors had settled in Poland some six or seven hundred years before I was born, 1 knew only a few worlds of the Polish language. We lived in Warsaw on Krochmalna street, which might well have been called a ghetto. Actually the

Jews of Russian-occupied Poland were free to live wherever they chose. I was an anachronism in every way, but I didn't know it, just as I didn't know that my friendship with Shosha, the daughter of our neighbour Bashele and her husband Zelig had anything to do with love". (P.3)

These lines reflect that this piece of fiction is written by a person who is a traditional Jew. Isaac Bashevis Singer is a traditional Jew person who has reflected all the Jewish traditions and customs in Shosha. His awareness of being Jewish is very strong.

> "Her father (Shosha's), Zelig, worked in a leather
> store. He left home early in the morning and
> returned late in the evening. His black beard was
> always short and round, and the Hasidim in our
> building said that he had it trimmed - a violation of
> Hasidic practice. He wore a short gaberdine, a stiff
> collar, a tie, and kid shoes with rubber tops.
> Saturday he went to a synagogue frequented by
> tradesmen and workers." (P. 4)

The protagonist is so keen about his culture that he observes every person and also sees that each person follows the religious practices or not. Aaron has a friendship with Shosha, but he observes her father also.

> "Though Bashele wore a wig, she did not shave her
> head as did my mother, the wife of Rabbi Menahem
> Mendl Greidinger. Mother often told me it was
> wrong for a rabbis son, a student of the Germara,
> to be the companion of a girl, and one from a
> common home at that. She warned me never to taste

anything there, since Bashele might feed me meat
that was not strictly Kosher" (P. 5)

Aaron's mother takes care of her son fearing that he
will go out of rituals. He is son of rabbi, a priest, so he has
got an important place in the society. His mother doesn't
allow him to meet a common girl like Shosha and nor does
she allow him to visit her house, because she fears that
Bashele, Shosha's mother might give him meat to eat that
is not strictly Kosher. Singer has mentioned all the Jewish
religious customs and rituals here with the help of which we
can locate the culture very easily.

> "On Sabbaths we weren't allowed to touch a candle
> stick, a coin, any of the things we amused ourselves
> with. Father reminded us constantly that this world
> was corridor in which one had to study the Torah
> and perform virtuous deeds, so that when one made
> one's way to the place that was the next world,
> rewards would be waiting to be collected". He used
> to say, "How long does one live, anyhow? Before
> you turn around its' all over. When a person, sins,
> his sins turn into devils, demons, hobgoblins. After
> death they chase the corpse and drag it through
> forsaken forests and deserts where people do not
> go or cattle tread". (P. 6)

Jewish philosophy about life and life after death depicts
in the above lines. It is very important to note here that, this
philosophy is given by a rabbi. The Jews are not beautiful
rather they are ugly. This is a great misunderstanding
throughout the world. Aaron, as a child was singled out

in particular because he was a rabbi's son and wore a long gaberdine and a velvet cap. The boys taunted him with names like "Fancypants". "Little Rabbi", "Mollycoddle", and they heard him speaking to Shosha, they jeered and called him "Sissy". He was also teased for having red hair, blue eyes and unusually white skin. (P. 6)

Only because Aaron was a rabbi's son and fair looking other children teased him. Aaron also went to Synagogue regularly. He boasted to the children that he was familiar with the Cabala and knew expressions so sacred that they could draw wine from the wall, create live pigeons and let people fly to Madagascar. One such name he knew contained seventy two letters, and when it was uttered the sky would turn red, the moon topple, and the world be destroyed.

Aaron was given different types of religions and other kind of books to read in his childhood. Singer has sketched this character is such a manner that is consists of all the things which locate the Jewish culture. "There stood on our Shelves volumes of the "Zohar", "The Tree of life", "The book of creation", "The Orchard of Pomegranates" and other 'Cabalistic' works. I found a calendar where many facts about kings, statesmen, millionnaires, and scholars were set down. My Mother often read "The Book of the Covenant" which was an anthology packed with scientific information.

Not only Aaron's father, but his mother was also religious by nature and read all the religious books. Being a son of a rabbi Jewish culture was an integral part of Aaron's life. A day did not pass without Aaron's coming to Shosha with new stories. He had discovered a potion that, if one drank it, it made him as strong as Samson. Aaron had drunk it already and was so strong that he could drive the Turks from the Holy Land and become king of the Jews; he had found a cap that, if someone put it on head, it made him invisible. He was about to grow as wise as King Soloman, who could speak the language of birds. He told Shosha about the Queen of Sheba, who came to learn wisdom from King Solomon and brought with her many slaves as well as camels and donkeys bearing gifts for the ruler of Israel. Aaron as a child had great impact of Jewishness on him. He always dreamt of becoming King of the Jews and promised Shosha that when he will become king, he will always have time for her. And Shosha will sit near him on the throne and rest her feet on a footstool of topaz. When the Messiah will come, all Jews will mount a cloud and fly to the Holy land. The Gentiles will become salves to the Jews and the daughter of the general will wash her feet. (P. 10)

Though Aaron was son of a rabbi, people were always ready to point out his mistakes. The members of the community that paid his father his weekly remuneration were watchful always ready to find some sign of misconduct in his children. (P. 11)

The second world war has a great impact on the Jewish culture. The smooth life of the Jews was totally disturbed by this unwanted event. Singer has given the worse conditions that followed after the war; "At home we soon began to go hungry. In the time between the assassination in Sarajevo and the outbreak of the war many wealthy housewives had stocked their larders with flour, rice, beans and groats but my mother had been busy reading morality books. Besides we had no money. The Jews on our street stopped paying my father. There were no more weddings, divorces or law suits in his courtroom. Long lines formed at the bakeries for a loaf of bread. The prize of meat soared. In Yanash's Bazaar the slaughterers stood with knives in their hands, looking out for a woman with a chicken, a duck, or a goose,. The price of fowl went up from day to day. Herring could not be bought at all. Many housewives began to use cocoa butter instead of butter. There was lack of kerosene. After the Succoth holiday the rains, the snow, the frosts began, but we couldn't afford coal for heating the oven. My brother Moishe stopped going to Cheder because his shoes were torn father became his teacher. Weeks passed by and we never tasted meat, not even on the Sabbath. We drank watery tea without sugar. We learned from the news papers that the Germans and Austrians had invaded many towns and villages in Poland among them those were where our relatives lived. The Czar's great uncle Nikolai Nikolaievitch, the chief commander, decreed that all Jews be driven from the regions behind the front; they were considered German spies. The Jewish streets in Warsaw teemed with thousands of refugees. They slept in the study houses, even in the Synagogues. It wasn't long before we began to hear to the shooting of heavy guns. The Germans attacked at the river Bzura, and the Russians launched a counterattack. In our apartment the windowpanes rattled day and night". (P. 12)

After the world war, it become very difficult for the Jews to follow their culture and their traditions. They were put in rehabilitation camps. Aaron was also put in such type of a camp but he was not sure that his Jewish purity will be protected there "There they shaved off my earlocks and fed me soup flavoured with pork. For me the son of a rabbi-these were spiritual calamities. A Gentile nurse ordered me to strip naked and gave me a bath. When she lathered me, her fingers tickled and I felt like both laughing and crying. It must be that I had fallen into the hands of the demonic Lilith dispatched by her husband, Asmodeus, to corrupt Yeshiva students and drag them down into the abyss of defilement. Later when I saw myself in a mirror and caught a glimpse of my image minus earlocks and ritual garment and wearing some kind of bathrobe 1 had never seen on a Jewish lad and slippers with wooden soles, I didn't recognize myself. I was no longer formed in the image of God". (P. 13)

After the world war Aaron faced a great blow. This blow was on his religion, spirituality and also on culture. Being a son of a rabbi and a true Jew, he was strictly brought up on the traditional Jewish rituals, but the world war made him suffer the worst things in his life. With the German soldiers Enlightenment had invaded Krochmalna 'street'. Aaron had heard of Darwin and was no longer sure that the miracles described in "The Assembly of Saints" had really occurred even since war had broken out on the Ninth Day of Ab, the Yiddish newspaper was brought daily into our house and he read about Zionism, Socialism, and following the Russian evacuation of Poland when the Russian censorship ceased, a series of articles about Rasputin. After the world war his world changed and he was slowly moving away from the Jewish culture.

Dora Stolnitz with whom Aaron had his first affair was a socialist. But Aaron was anti-communist anti all "isms" - but he lived in constant fear of being arrested and imprisoned because of her. Aaron believed that the aim of literature was to prevent time from vanishing but his own time, he threw away. The twenties had passed and the thirties had come.

Hitler was fast becoming the ruler of Germany. In Russia the purges had commenced. In Poland, 'Pilsudski had created a military dictatorship. Years earlier America consulates of nearly all nations refused to issue visas to Jews. Aaron was stranded in a country squeezed between two mighty foes, stuck, with a language and culture no one recognized outside of a small circle of Yiddishists and radicals. But he found friends among members of the winter's club and it's periphery. Aaron was the son of a rabbi, but he had fled the house and became an agnostic. He divorced three wives and constantly changed lovers. Morris Feitelzohn, one of Aaron's friends constantly read "The Duty of the Hearts, The Path of the Righteous" and other Hasidic books. He once said to Aaron, "I love the Jews even though I cannot stand them. No evolution could have created them. For they are the only proof of God's existence". (P. 19)

Aaron has a great fear of the Nazis as all the Jews had. He says that cubism and expressionism had been in fashion many years, but Haiml liked pastoral landscapes of woods, meadows, streams, and huts half hidden behind trees, where, as he put it, once could hide from Hiter, who was threatening to invade Poland and 'Aaron himself had fantasies about a house in the woods or on an island where he could be safe from Nazis. He was a writer, but he couldn't understand about what to write. Twenty million people had perished in the Great war, and here the world was preparing for another conflagration. And she felt that what he could write about that wasn't already known? A new style? Every experiment with words turned quickly into a collection of mannerisms. (P.25)

Anti-semitism was so strong that Rachel a Jewish actress was pushed out of Paris by anti-semites. Aaron's father was a scholoar-a Hasid, a follwer of the Husiatiner rabbi and the Bolsheviks shot him. He was rich one, but the war had ruined him His whole family stayed on in Russia but he couldn't remain among the murderers of his father.

The threat of second world war was always there on the Jews. The newspapers talked of how modern the German Army had become, fully mobilized and equipped with the latest weapons, but the Polish soldiers looked just like the Russian soldiers in 1914. They wore heavy faces. Their rifles appeared too long and too bulky. All of them were doomed to be massacred, yet they made fun of the Jews in the long gabardines. One even tugged at a Jew's beard, and they could be heard hissing' "Zydy, Zydy, Zydy". (P. 67) when Aaron was travelling with Betty and Sam, he saw this cruel picture.

In Germany Hitler has solidified his power, but the Warsaw Jews were so strong about their culture that they celebrated the festival of the exodus out of Egypt four thousand years ago. Aaron was also strict about Jewish culture, when Betty brought a bouquet for him & Tekla his maid servant put it in a vase, he was very surprised, because he had never heard of woman bringing flowers for a man.

When Aaron takes Betty to see his old place where he stayed previously, Betty, an American actress could not withstand the stinking place. But Aaron had many memories there and besides, he also meets Shosha after a long period of time. Betty understands that Aaron is in love with Shosha & suggests him not to marry an insane girl like Shosha, because he will not bear children from her. Shosha's mother Bashele too feels happy after meeting, Aaron and asks him to wait for dinner, but Betty refuses. Sam drieman complained because Aaron wouldn't bathe with him in the little river. But Aaron was embarrassed about undressing before strangers. He had never freed himself from a nation inherited from generations: the body is a vessel of shame and disgrace, dust in life and worse in death. Celia wanted Aaron to leave Warsaw and stay at fresh outdoors, she argued that, "let's snatch a little peace before another world' war breaks out". (P. 90) This shows that the Jews were constantly under the fear of the war.

Aaron is so much under the pressure of culture and rituals that after a long period, he takes Shosha out on the streets but he didn't dare to bring her in Synagogue, he says" I didn't dare bring a girl into a Hasidic prayer house while the congregation was praying. Only on Simchas Torah were girls allowed inside a house of worship, or when a relative was deathly ill and the family gathered to pray before the holy ark". (P. 98) when Aaron is not able to write the play properly for Sam Drieman, he becomes very angry and shouts at Aaron saying that "if Jews where capable of such deceit and intrigue, then Hitler was right".

Aaron expreses his views freely about the Jews. "The Jews in Poland were trapped". When he said this in the writer's club, they attacked him. They had let themselves fall into a stupid kind of optimism, but Aaron knew that for sure they all are going to be destroyed. The Poles wanted to get rid of the Jews. They considered them nation within a nation, a strange and malignant body. They lack the courage to finish off the Jews; but they wouldn't shed tears if Hitler did it for them. Stalin will certainly not defend the Jews.

Since the Trotskyite opposition began the communists have become their (Jew's) worst enemies. Trotosky is called Judas in Russia. The fact is the Trotskyites are almost all Jews. "If you give a Jew one revolution, he demands another revolution a permanent one. If you give him one Messiah, he asks for another revolution a permanent one. As to Palestine the world doesn't want the Jews to have 'a state. The bitter truth is that many Jews today don't want to be Jews any more. But it's too late for total assimilation. Whoever is going to win this coming war will liquidate the Jews. (P. 131)

There was a kind of phobia about America among the Jews. Fietelzohn represents the worldwide view about America in the following words.

"If one lives in America a few years, one becomes an American. What would the world do without America? When lived there I complained of Uncle Sam steadily talked only about his shortcomings. But now that I am here, I miss America. I could go back if I chose, on a tourist visa. It might even be that I could get a visa as a professor. But in New York and Boston no University would give me a permanent job. And to teach in those small colleges somewhere in the midwest means dying of boredom. I cannot sit all day long and read like a bookworm. The students there are more childlike than our Cheder boys. All they talk about is football, and the professors are not much cleverer. America is a country of children. The New Yorkers are a little more grown up, but not much. Once some friend of mine put me on a ferry to Coney Island. This, Tsutsik, I wish you could see. It is a city in which everything in for play-shooting at tin ducklings, visiting a museum. Where they show a girl with two heads, letting an astrologer plot your horoscope and a medium call up the soul of your grandfather in the beyond. No place lacks vulgarity, but the vulgarity of Coney Island is of special kind friendly with a tolerance that says. "I play my game and you play your game. As I walked around there and ate a hot dog- this is what they call a sausage it occurred to me that 1 was seeing the future of mankind. You can even call it the time of the Messiah. One day all people will realize that there is not a single idea that can really be called true - that everything is a game, nationalism, internationalism, religion, atheism, spiritualism, materialism even suicide.

Fietelzohn as a Jew gives the simple principle of humanity which most of the human beings don't follow. He says that the basis of ethics is man's right to play the game of his choice. I will not trample on your toys and you will not trample on mine, I won't spit on your idol and you will not spite on mine. There is no reason why hedonism, the Cabala, polygamy, ascetism, even our friend Haiml's blend of eroticism and Hasidism could not exist in a play city or play world a sort of a Universal Coney Island where everyone would play according to his or her desire. I am sure Miss Slonim that you have visited 'Coney Island more than once. (P. 135)

When Aaron tells Fietelzohn about Shosha, he says "Shosha ? A modern girl with such on old fashioned name ? What is she, a fighting Yiddishist?" (P. 136) He thinks that Aaron is a writer and a modern man so he will marry a modern girl. But he doesn't know that Aaron is very much keen about his childhood sweetheart Shosha. Aaron's life is full of ups and downs. When Celia wants to tell the truth about Shosha to Feitelzohn he says that "whenever I expect life to remain status quo, something unexpected pops up.

World history is made of the some dough as bagels, it must be fresh. This is why democracy and capitalism are going down the drain. They have become state. This is the reason idolatry was so exciting. You could buy a new God every year, we Jews burdened the nations with an eternal God, and therefore they hate us. Gibbon tried so hard to find the reason for the fall of the Roman Empire. It fell only because it had become old. I hear that there is a passion for newness in the sky also. A star gets tired of being a star and it explodes and becomes old. I hear that there is a passion for newness in the sky also. A star gets tired of being a star and it explodes and becomes a nova. The milky way got weary of its sour milk, and began to run to the devil knows where. (P. 137)

Feitelzohn asks whether Shosha is a sick girl and Aaron answers "when the body gets tired of being healthy, it become sick when it gets tired of living, it dies. When it has enough of being dead, it reincarnates into a frog or a windmill." (P. 137) Betty Slonim is an actress therefore she wants to be young always. So, when Feitelzohn calls her Miss Slonim she requests him not to call her so, but call as Betty.

Shosha's mother Bashele follows all the Jewish rituals. Two days before Yom Kippur eve, she bought two hens with which to perform the sacrificial ceremony, one for herself and the other for Shosha. She wanted to buy a rooster for Aaron also, but he refused to let a rooster die for his sins. Certain writers in the Yiddish newspaper had come out against this rite, calling it idolatrous. The Zionist supporters proposed sacrificing money instead, which would go to the Jewish national fund for Palestine. Still, from all the apartments on Krochamalna street one could hear the clucking of hens and the crowing of roosters. Jews keep on wishing eternal life, or at least immortality of the soul. In fact, eternal life would be a calamity. If they forget the past they are no longer the same. And if they remember all of the pettiness of life then they cannot grow.

Sam Drieman wants Aaron to leave Poland & settle in America. He tries to convince Aaron by saying that, "Things will not end well in Poland. That beast Hitler will soon come with his Nazis. There will be great war. Americans will lend a hand and they will do what they did in the last war but before that the Nazis will attack the Jews and there will be nothing but grief for you here. The Yiddish papers are in trouble already, there was no book publisher and what goes on the stage is disgusting. How will you make a living ? A writer has to eat, too. Even Moses had to eat. That's what the holy books say. (P. 155) He even asks Aaron to Marry Betty, but Aaron is a Jew, moreover he loves Shosha. He thinks that from the time he reached manhood he had told himself that he would marry a girl just like his mother a decent, chaste Jewish daughter. He always felt pity for men with dissolute wives. He thinks seriously over the proposal of Sam and his conscious hits him. A voice from inside him says, "Don't shame me your mother, and your holy ancestors ! All you deeds are noted in heaven". Then the voice began to abuse him. "Heathen ! Betrayer of Israel ! See what happens when you deny the Almighty ! You shall utterly abhor it, for it is a cursed thing!"

Once Aaron went to a barber's shop for cutting his hair. And the barber who was a non-Jew expressed his sharp views against the Jews while cutting. Aaron's hair "I will tell you something, dear sir. The modern Jews, those who shave, who speak a proper Polish and who try to ape real Poles, are even worse than the old fashioned Hebes with their long gaberdines, wild beards and earlocks. They, at least don't go where they aren't wanted. They sit in their stores in their long capotes and shake over their Talmud like Bedouins. They babble away in their jargon, and when a Christian falls into their clutches they swindle a few groschen out of him. But at least they don't go to the theatre the cafes, the opera. Those that shave and dress modern are the real danger. They sit in our Sejm and make treaties with our worst enemies the Ruthenians, the white Russians, the Lithuanians. Every one of them is a secret communist and a Soviet spy. They have one aim- to root out the Christians and hand over the power to the Bolsheviks the Masons, and the radicals. You might find it hard to believe this, dear sir, but their millionaires have a secret pact with Hitler. His real name isn't Roosevelt but Rosenfeld, a converted Jew, they supposedly assume the Christian Jew, They supposedly assume the Christian faith, but with one goal in mind to bore from within and infect everything and everybody. Funny don't you think?" Aaron emitted a half continued... They come here for a shave and a haircut all year, but not today. Yom Kippur is a holy day even for those that are rich and modern. More than half the stores are closed here and on Marshal Kowska street. They don't go to the Hasidic prayer houses in fur-edged hats and prayer shawls like the old fashioned sheenis- Oh no, they put on top hats and drive to the synagogue on Tlomacka street in private cars. But Hitler will clean them out! He promises their millionaires that he will protect their capital, but once the Nazis are armed he will fix them all ha, ha, ha! It's too bad that he will attack our country, but since we haven't had the guts to sweep away this filth ourselves, we have to let the enemy do it for us. What will happen later, no one can know. The fault for it all lies with those traitors, the Protestants, who sold their souls to the devil. They are the Pope's deadliest enemies. Did you know dear sir, that Luther was a secret Jew ?"

The barber spoke everything which the anti Jews felt. He didn't think even that Aaron must be a Jew, because Aaron went to cut his hairs on Yom Kippur. In Warsaw, everywhere there was a fear of Hitler and war. Tekla, a maid also fears from war but she feels that wars are unnecessary. She says the best thing they find to say is that if there were no wars, no epidemics, and no famines, people would multiply like rabbits and there soon woudn't be enough for everybody to eat. She asks innocently to Aaron that "doesn't rye grow in the fields for bread?". Why didn't God make it so there would be enough for all?" But Aaron answers that he is not able to answer these questions. Because nobody in the world can answer why wars take place? Even God cannot answer this question. The philosophy of Gandhi is accepted by the world. Even Singer has mentioned Gandhi in Shosha. "At the time of war America had locked its gates and England, France, Canada, Australia - all the capitalists countries did the same. In India thousands of people die of hunger each day. 'English travellers admit this themselves. When Gandhi submissive as he is, uttered a word, they threw him in jail. It this true or not? Gandhi babbles about passive resistance. What a swindle ! How can resistance be passive ? It's exactly as if you would say hot snow, cold fire" (P. 181). A revolutionary explains Aaron the need for war by giving the example of India, where Gandhi the worshipper of peace was put behind bars.

Often Aaron Greidinger feels guilty for not following the Jewish customs and rituals thoroughly. Likewise, Dora also feels the same and once she expresses it before Aaron. "From the day I had left my father's house I had existed in a state of perpetual despair. Occasionally, I considered the notion of repentance, of returning to real Jewishness. But to live like my father, my grandfathers and great grandfathers without their faith- was this possible ? Each time I went into a library, I felt a spark of hope that perhaps in one of the books there might be some indication of how a person of my disposition and world outlook could make peace with himself I didn't find not in it- not in Tolstory or in Kropot Kin, not in Spinoza or in William James, not in Schopenhaver, not in the scriptures. Certainly the prophets preached a high morality but their promises of plentiful harvests, of fruitful olive tress and Vinenyards, protection against one's enemies, made no appeal to me. 1 knew that the world had always been and would always remain as it was now. What the moralists called evil was actually the order of life" (P. 183)

This was the plight of every Jew in Poland and in the world also. Aaron's mother and rabbi brother came to Warsaw for his marriage. His mother follows strictly Jewishness, When the proprietor of boarding house asks her about breakfast she asks whether it was strictly kosher. And he answers that even the rabbis ate there. His mother is an intelligent lady. A girl is not allowed to study Torah, but she stood behind the door and listened, as Aaron's grandfather lectured to the Yeshiva boys. And if one of them made a mistake, she knew it well. According to her no one knows what heaven wants. If God had wanted the Jews to live, He wouldn't have created Hitlers.

Shosha's mother intended to invite his mother for lunch or supper but she told Aaron plainly she wouldn't eat in Bashele's house. Neither she nor Moishe had confidence that the food in her kitchen was strictly Kosher. However, she and Moishe agreed to go for tea and fruit.

At Bashele's house neighbours and old women gathered to meet Aaron's mother, wife of the late rabbi. And there was a discussion on the then condition in Warsaw and the old memories came out. "Hitler- his name should be blotted out is not the only Villain. There are Hitlers in every city, in every community. If we forget the lord for a second, we are immediately on the side of defilement. (P. 198) This was the feeling of those old women who came to meet Aaron.

Aaron marries Shosha & after that they decide to visit Otwock. While travelling in the train, Shosha forgets her pillow, and starts crying because of that. The conductor saw this and asked Aaron whether she was his daughter. And Aaron doesn't understand what to say. But indeed Aaron loves and takes care of Shosha like a small child.

Shosha dies. And why she died, even Aaron couldn't understand. After thirteen years when he again comes to Warsaw from New York he is forty three and tries to find his old days with the help of fifty plus Haiml. From Haiml he comes to know that Celia was also no more. The war had ruined the Jews of Poland. And Haiml says "well a Jewish land, a Jewish sea. Who would have believed this ten years age? Such a thought was beyond daring. All our dream centered around a crust of bread, a plate of groats, a clean shirt. Fietelzohn once said something I often repeat: "A man has no imagination either in his pessimism or his optimism". Who could have figured that the Gentiles would vote for a Jewish nation? Nu, but the birth throes are far from over. The Arabs haven't made peace with the situation. It's hard here. Thousands of refuges live in tin shacks. I lived in. one of them myself. The sun roasts you all day like fire, and at night you freeze. The women are at each other's throats. Refugees have come from Africa who have never seen a handkerchief - literally people from Abraham's time. Who knows what they are, maybe descendant of Keturah. I hear you have become famous in America" (P.266)

Haiml marries a woman who had lost her husband and children in the gas chamber. Betty married an American Army colonel & then she committed suicide. Teibele ran away to Russia with her married boyfriend, a shopkeeper and Aaron's mother and brother died in the forest of Russia in a cold winter and what happened to Bashele Aaron didn't knew. In this manner the war scattered all the loved ones from each other and gave a permanent scar on the heart of the Jews.

E) The Kabbalic basis of Singer's secular vision:

The Kabbalah which simply means "tradition", is a collective term for a variety of esoteric teachings based on the Torah which has developed for generations by Jewish mystics.[6.] Singer uses the religious thoughts of the ancient Kabbalah to explore the godless vision of the modern world and in doing so, he maintains in his fiction a precarious balance between the Biblical[7] and the secular between belief and disbelief. One of the concerns central to the Kabbalah is the nature of God's presence in creation. The Zohar, which is the major Kabbalic text, consisting of several volumes of homilies, commentaries and expositions on the Torah refers to God as "Ein-Sof", an inaccessible unknowable infinite whose existence it is possible to deduce only through the existence of creation.[8] This hidden God manifests itself in creation by means often sefirot, which are referred to as attributes of Einsof, or its epithets- Ein- sof's calling forth of its sefirot in the process of creating the world, the world is conceived of as a revelation of its hidden being or as the articulation of its hidden essence into divine speech.

However, that vision of the Zohar which became the preeminent text for the culture of Singer's childhood, Polish Hasidism, emphasized not the presence of Ein-Sof in the world but rather its exile from the world. This text was developed in the sixteenth century by Rabbi Isaac Luria, one of a small group of religious thinkers in Safed, a Palestinian village. The Safed group, profoundly influenced by the catastrophic expulsion of the Jews from Spain a generation earlier, in 1492, refined the Kabbalah in crucial ways. They interwove the historical experience of the exile of the Jewish people with a mystical understanding of the Universe, so that at the heart of the Kabbalah "lay a great image of rebirth, the myth of exile and redemption.

The Lurianic Kabbalah reveals exile to be the condition of the universe and even of God-Luria describes creation not as the progressive manifestation of Ein-Sof through emanations but rather as a twofold act, the first of which creates a chasm between God and the world. In Lurianic doctirne, Ein-Sof was not revealed in the initial act of creation, but rather was concealed so that the world could be revealed. Only then did Ein-Sof create the world through emanations. The first action in creation called trimtzum, or contraction, is given great emphais by Luria, becoming a metaphor of divine exile. Simply put, God filled all space and had to contract 'inward to make a place for creation; or as it is variously explained, God's radiance filled all space, so that the light had to be dimmed to make a place for creation'.

The second stage of the Lurianic creation myth extends the idea of God's exile from the world. After removing itself from the place of creation, Ein-Sof began the process of emanation, 'sending the sefirot, sometimes imagined as rays of divine light into the space provided for creation. Through the sefirot, Ein-Sof created the cosmos and everything in it. During the process of emanation the Kabbalists tell us, the sefirot entered vessels in order to take from, but the vessels could not contain the light and therefore broke. The divine light was scattered throughout creation. Nothing is where it should be all being is in exile.

In a sense, God too through the sefirot was dispersed thoughtout the world. Luria, countering the pantheistic implications of the doctrine of emanation, posited a curtain or wall between the world of divinity and the world of creation. The curtain refracts the divine substances back into itself, while it allows a radiance to filter through. Thus, "not En-Sof itself is dispersed in the nether worlds, but only a radiance". Luria's clarification serves to underscore once more the exile and inaccessibility of God. Creation is God's Cosmic exile. Paradoxically, God is both nowhere and yet his radiance is everywhere dispersed. Thus, throughout their lives Singer's characters have intimations of transcendence, fleeting moments of clarity when they seem to have touched upon a larger truth, but these moments can never be sustained; "they are as intricate and hidden as crown of feathers.

The implied yet inaccessible God of the Kabbalists becomes, in Singer's hands a hidden and perhaps altogether absent God whose very existence is open to question. Out of the ancient religious tradition to which he is heir, Singer forms a modern secular vision. He shifts the emphasis of the Kabbalic creation story, transforming the Zohar from a system of belief into a prescription for doubt. His work accentuates which suggest that the very existence of the world is predicated upon the absence of God from it. As a soul in the soul in the first sphere of heaven remarks. "He is supposed to dwell in the seventh heaven, which is an infinity away, one thing we can be sure of, he is not her". "Before Ain Sof created the world he first dimmed his light void.

It was only in this void that the emanation commenced. This divine absence may be the very essence of creation". (P. 51).

In Singer's work, the God we find is one who has created a world devoid of the possibility of God. We are teased with hints of transcendence only to be reminded that the world exists in the absence of any such transcendence. The mere mention of "God" in a Singer creation then serves not to affirm a traditional religious transcendence as it is so often presumed to do, but rather to suggest cosmic exile, inscrutability, concealment, and silence it evokes a universe which remains a riddle a teasing puzzle which we long to comprehend but never can.

It is paradoxical vision of God as both present in and absence from creation, the Zohar simultaneously offers possibilities for both belief and disbelief. In "Shosha", Singer holds these possibilities in a precarious balance. Aaron, a believer who extends his willingness to believe to every aspect of his life, is tempted to disbelieve the stories told to him to deny his faith and to enact revenge against those who humiliate him for his gullibility. Aaron builds his life upon belief. "Belief in itself is beneficial", he follows this policy. Extending that faith to all the creation, Aaron ignores that Shosha is not a suitable match for him. Though his narrative strategy, Singer transforms this simple tale of temptation into a sophisticated dialect in which, while Aaron wants to move steadfastly in the path of faith, the reader is pushed along a counterpath of skepticism and disbelief until the paths cross and both character and reader must face the central question of faith; neither the paradoxes of faith in the Zohar nor the crisis of faith in "Shosha" are ever resolved. Singer brings his reader to an unresolved crisis of faith in order to define the human being as one who is confronted by the question of ultimate meaning as a baffling problem and as one who is in exile from any resolution to that problem.

In Hasidic culture, the murmuring of words in prayer is considered in and of itself a holy action because uttering the word constitutes an imitation of God's creative act, while fiction is considered to be a blasphemous use of the sacred word, which should be used only to explicate holy texts or to tell the holy people. But Singer, exploiting the implications of the Sefer Yezirah's image of God as writer, reveals storytelling to be as much an imitation of the primal creative act as is prayer and fiction to be as much an imitation of the primal creative act as is prayer and fiction to be as much as source of truth as is faith.

Although rendered in archaic diction and often times associated with astrology and magic, particularly with the magical power of letters and words, the linguistic theory of the Kabbalah is surprisingly modern in its implications. The idea that language creates reality, that existence may be a dream or a text; and that we may be more characters within the text is a theme which not only Singer but Borges, Nabokov, Fowles, Coover, Barth and other modern fiction writers play with repeatedly. It undermines the primacy of empirical reality, rendering both reality and our own existence tentative, subject perhaps to the whim of an author's offhand remark. Hasidic legend holds that before creating the world, God created and destroyed, like so many rough drafts seven others. Singer in imitation of his absent God fills the void with fictional worlds, creating and recreating until the Universe becomes a magical collage of new texts, each vying with God's original for creative primary. Singer's play with realities which although alien to one another, seem to intersect and thus to call into question their own substantiality, further undermines the assumption that a stable world order, an absolute reality exists. Reality becomes plural and amorphous.

It is to literature then, that we look not only for a depiction of an art but also for the hope, inherent in the Kabbalic conception of language, that through words we may create new sources of meaning. The idealization if luggage, so prevalent in the sensibilities of modern writers and so ancient in its. Source while wreaking much havoc upon empiricism, raises the imagination to sublime heights.

If language is sacred, if its hidden essence is truth, then its imaginative acts are preludes to revelation; here again for Singer, faith and fiction converge.

Conclusion:

Beneath the surface of simple folktale, "Shosha" an elaborate process is seen wherein the dynamics of fiction are tightly joined with the assumptions of faith and culture. Singer, in the most modern of manners, manipulates fictional conventions to further his thematic considerations and posits a new transcendence based, not upon the supernatural but upon the infinite possibilities of language and the imagination. Storytelling itself is a motif which runs throughout the fiction. Singer's fiction overflows with a cacophony of narrative voices- whispering, gossiping, sharing secret stories. In tales with contemporary setting, narrators in varying degrees rather closely resembling the author himself, are writers of note who share stories with us or are pursued by those obsessed with sharing theirs.

For Singer, storytelling is a significant action, rooted in the primal act of creation and associated with the linguistic theories of the Kabbalah. Often he makes playful allusions to these associations. In "Shosha" the life of Jews during and after war is shown. "Shosha' trace the characteristic motions of human destiny, a heavy climb upward, a rapid tumble down ward. Life forms a journeying to heaven and hell, mostly hell. What determines the direction a man will take? Sometimes the delicate maneouvres between his will and desire, sometimes the heat of his vanity, sometimes the blessing of innocence. But more often than not it is all mystery which Singer chooses to present rather than explain. As his figures move upward of their ineluctable destiny, they stop for a moment in the shtetl world. Singer is not content with the limitations of materiality, yet not at all indifferent to the charms and powers of the phenomenal universe. In his calculus of destiny, however, the world is a resting place and what happens within it, even within the social enclave of the Jews, is not of lasting significance. Thick, substantial, and attractive as it comes to seem in Singer's representation, the world is finally but lure and appearance, a locale between heaven and hell, the shadow of larger possibilities.

In most Yiddish fiction the stress is quite different. There the central "character" is the collective destiny of the Jews in galut or exile; the central theme, the survival of a nation deprived of nationhood; the central ethic, the humane education of men stripped of worldly power yet sustained by the memory of closeness and the promise of redemption. In Singer, the norm of collective life is still present where culture can be located but mostly in the background as a tacit assumption; his major actions break away from the limits of the shtetl ethic, what has come to be known as "Yiddish Keit", and then move either backward to the abandon of false messianism or forward to the doubt of modern sensibility.

The historical settings of East European Jewish life are richly presented in "Shosha" often not as orderly sequences in time but simulataneous perceptions jumbled together in the consciousness of figures for whom Abraham's sacrifice, Chmielnicki's pogroms, the rise and fall of Hasidism and the stirrings of the modern world are all felt with equal force. Yet Singer's ultimate concern is not with the collective experience of a chosen or martyred people but with the enigmas of personal fate. Given the slant of his vision, this leads him to place a heavy reliance upon the grotesque as mode of narration, even as an avenue towards knowledge. But the grotesque carries with it a number of literary and moral dangers, not the least being the tempatation for Singer to make it into an end in itself, which is to say, something facile and sensationalistic. Mainly the grotesque succeeds in Singer's writings because it comes to symbolize meaningful digressions from a cultural norm. An uninstructed reader may absorb Singer's grotesquerie somewhat too easily into the assumptions of modern literature; the reader who grasps the ambivalence of Singer's relation to Yiddish literature will see the grotesquire as a cultural sign by means of which singer defines himself against his own past.

It is hardly a secret that in the Yiddish literary world Singer is regarded with a certain suspicion. His powers of evocation, his resources as a stylist are acknowledged, yet many Yiddish literary person, including the serious ones seem uneasy about him. One reason is that "modernism" - which, as these people regard Singer, signifies a heavy stress upon sexuality, a concern for the irrational, expressionist distortions of character, and a seeming indifference to the humane ethic of Yiddishism - has never won so strong a hold in Jewish culture as it has in the culture of most western countries. For the Yiddish writers, 'modernism' has been at best an adornment of manner upon a subject inescapably traditional.

Within his limits Singer is a genius. He has total command of his imagined world, he is original in his use both of traditional Jewish materials and his modernist attitude towards them; he provides a series of enigmatic moral perspective, and he is a master of Yiddish prose. To this buried strand of Jewish experience Singer has been drawn in fascination and repulsion, potraying its manifestations with great vividness and its consequences with stern judgement. It is a kind of experience that rarely figures in traditional Yiddish writing yet is a significant aspect of the Jewish past. Bringing this material to contemporary readers, Singer writes in Yiddish but often quite apart from the Yiddish tradition. Indeed, he is one of the few Yiddish writes whose relation to the Jewish past is not determined or screened by that body of values we call Yiddishism.

Glossary

1. Chanukah - Holiday celebrating rededication of the Temple in Jerusalem in 165 B. C. E.

2. Diaspora - From the Greek for "disperation" that is the Jews living outside the Holy Land.

3. Dybbuk - A condemned spirit who inhabits the body of a living person and controls his or her actions.

4. Ein-Sof - Literally, "without end", a Cabalistic term for that aspect of the godhead about which nothing can be thought or said.

5. Eretz Israel - The land of Israel

6. Galut - Exile, condition of Jewish people in exile.

7. Gemarah   - Section of the Talmud interpreting the mishnah.

8. Goy   - A gentile, a non- Jew; literally, Hebrew for 'nation'

9. Halakhah   - That part of Jewish literature which deals with religious, ethical, civil, and criminal law.

10. Hasidim   - Religious, enthusiasts, devotes of Hasidism, or "pietism", a religious revival beginning in the 18th century.

11. Kaddish   - Literally "Sanctification", but usually refers to ceremonial prayer for the dead.

12. Lamed - Vov - Hebrew for the number 36; according to a statement in the Talmud (Sanhedrin 97b), "the world must contain not less than 36 righteous men vouchsafed the sight of the Divine Presence".

13. Mishnah   - Earliest codification of the oral law, which is the basis of the Talmud.

14. Passover   - Festival of unleavened bread, commemorating the exodus of the children of Israel from Egypt.

15. Purim   - Holiday commemorating the deliverance of the Jews of Persia from destruction as told in the biblical book of Esther.

16. Rebbetsin   - Wife of a Rabbi or teacher.

17. Schlemiel — A foolish and powerless but sometimes also wise and saintty individual.

18. Sefirot — Literally "number" in Hebrew, plural form of sefira; Cabalistic term for emanations and mainfestations of the godhead.

19. Shechinah — Divine presence.

20. Shevuot — Feast of the Pentecost; festival commemorating the giving of the Torah to Moses.

21. Shtetl — Jewish town or village of Eastern Europe.

22. Shulchan Aruch — 'Prepared Table', standard code of Jewish law compiled by Joseph Karo and first published in 1565.

23. Simachat Torah — "Rejoicing of the Law", a holiday celebration.

24. Talmud — Result and record of eight centuries of study and discussion of the Bible by Jewish scholars in the academics of Palestine and Babylonia.

25. Torah — Narrowly, the Pentateuch, but by extension all Jewish teaching.

26. Yeshiva — Institute for higher learning in Judaism.

27. Yom Kippur — Day of Atonement.

Notes:

1. (A citation by Swedish Academy)
   Ann Evory (Ed), "Contemporary Authors", New Revision series', vol. I (Detroit Gale Research company, 1980.)P. 604.

2. Katha Politt,"Creators on Creating: Isaac Bashevis Singer", Saturday Review, Carl Tucker (ed), (New York, Penthouse Intl. Ltd, July 1980) P. 50.

3. Katha Politt, "Creators on Creating: Isaac Bashevis Singer" op. cit. p.

4. Ibid, P. 50.

5. Malcolm Bradbury, "Possibilities: Eassays on the State of the Novel" (Eondon; Oxford University Press, 1973), P. 12.

6. Grace Farrell Lee "From Exile to Redemption", The Fiction of Isaac Bashevis Singer (Southern Illinois University Press, Carbonadale and Edwards ville Pub.)P. 6.

7. Ibid, P. 10.

8. Ibid, P. 20.

Chapter - IV

CONCLUSION

Every writer writes out of a culture. That culture may be a battleground of conflicting visions and values, and the writer may either embrace or attack his cultural heritage. Saul Bellow is a modern Jewish writer who writes about modern Jew in his "The Victim" whereas I. B. Singer is an orthodox writer who writes about holocaust and the conditions after it in his "Shosha". Jewish tradition and Jewish history, especially centuries of dispersion, exile, precariousness, homelessness and powerlessness, gave rise to a distinct historical attitude towards humanity and heroes. What is glorified in Yiddish life and literature is intellectual pursuit, not for its own sake but, ideally, as a route to good, a means of understanding.

Much American - Jewish literature is about the sociological and psychological dimensions of Jewish life about being Jewish in America, and focusses on the Jew as Everyman- an ethnic one, but an everyman. But some of the writing has been more particular, more specifically Jewish, and has emphasized the Jewish quality by relying on Jewish roots and sources. As American - Jewish fiction insists on man's mixed nature, so it walks the middle line between optimism and pessimism, complete hopeful affirmation and despair. Centuries of persecution preclude easy optimism, while hope and faith, whether in God or in a progressive future, have kept Jews from despair. Not only is this vision balanced and moderate in its estimation of man and the future, but it is deeply suspicious of the extremes. Both nihilism and romanticism are seen as wrongheaded and dangerous. As the American - Jewish novelist are most interested in ideas and cultural questions, Bellow frequently takes the temperature of the culture and prescribes medication to eliminate fever or chill.

- Bellow Saul, The Victim, Penguin Books, 1947. All subsequent references to the text are from this edition.
- Singer I. B., Shosha, New York Farrar Straus and Giroux, 1978. All subsequeni references to the text are from this edition.

In post - world war II American - Jewish fiction, family is the crucial bond that links or chains people together. In this fiction, the family is the locus of narrative and the agent of meaning. From the earliest American Jewish literature until the most recent the family is the heart of human life. Intense family feeling is a major theme in Bellow's work. Certainly, family is not always depicted positively in contemporary American - Jewish fiction, but it is always central. Alfred kazin has remarked on "the age -old"[1] Jewish belief that the only possible salvation lies in thinking well, which is thinking one's way to the root of all creation, thinking one's way to the ultimate reason of things. The emphasis on intellect and reason pervades traditional Judaism, where knowledge of sacred texts and intellectual ability to analyse and discuss them marks of highest distinction. But in traditional Judaism the intellect is not a totally separate sphere, it is a partner of the spirit, a means to a spiritual ideal. The extra ordinary high rate of literacy and experience with its sophisticated traditions made Jewish immigrants to this country a distinct group. This is reflected in the earliest American - Jewish fiction. Contemporary American - Jewish fiction is full of intellectuals.

In American - Jewish fiction, time, history and memory define human life, makes us human. This time - drenched Universe is virtually opposite the mainstream of American literature and culture. While most American literature posits the United States as a new beginning, an Eden in which every man and every woman can see them selves as Adam and eve, Jewish memory is long and profound. For the Jewish imagination, Thoreau's ecstatic perpetual dawn is a terrifying amnesia, and the linked themes of time, history and memory pervade American - Jewish fiction. For example E. L. Doctorow's 'The Book of Daniel'[2] (1971) is about the growing historical sense and recovery of memory of the protagonist, Daniel Isaacson, and Jerome Wiedman's story, "My Father sits in the Dark" (1934), is about an immigrant Jew enveloping memories of his old country childhood and his native American son's incomprehension.

It is not surprising that the themes of history, memory, and time are frequently focussed on the most traumatic, devastating historical experience in modern Jewish history, the Holocaust American - Jewish writers have tended to avoid evoking the Holocaust directly and to repudiate the nihilism that it implicitly suggests.

Contemporary American - Jewish fiction writers who have written about the holocaust include Bellow and I. B. Singer among the other imminent ones. In general, American - Jewish fiction writers have written about the Holocaust by focussing on a survivor who has come to this country. In this way, they have struggled to bring together the American reality and European event, the unprecedented post war material ease and relative psychological well being on the one hand and the most unfathomable monstrous event in Jewish history on the other.

Just how decisive was America's environment in the holocaust can be distilled from a single episode in 1945. Standing above and pit containing the remains of countless death camp victims, General D wight D. Elsenhower directed his troops to scrutinize the destruction and the death all around.[3] "The starvation, cruelty and bestiality were so overpowering as to leave me a bit sick", he later recalled. But Eisen hower insisted on seeing the worst the camp had to offer, and he urged the American government to send reporters and congressmen because he wanted to "leave no room for cynical doubt."

Everything significant in Americas relationship to the Holocaust was symbolized in that scene.

a) The mandate to remember and the resistance to remembering and

b) The deep impression that the Holocaust would make on American (and American Jewish) life and culture.

The holocaust (Shoah), a disaster of biblical proportions for European Jewry, forced Jewish American literature to explore its impact on the world's largest Diaspora community. In the process, novelists both well and lesser known and representing a variety of orientations to Judaism, have come to reflect on the meaning of covenantal existence and Jewish identity.

While the Holocaust is the fundamental orienting event for contemporary Jewish existence, raising in an intense manner questions about God, chosenness and the nature of evil, Jewish American novelists were slow to make it the orienting theme of their fiction. Separated by geography, history and language from the agony of their slaughtered European brethren Jewish American novelists, with few exceptions, continued for almost two decades after the Holocaust to display pre-war modes of historical and theological innocence. They concerned themselves with issues such as assimilation and suburban Judaism or presented romanticized images of a vanished shtetl world. In the 1960 s, however, several events reminded Jews every where of their vulnerability. A plentitude of Holocaust novels and short stories emerged against this background, reflecting a growing awareness of the Holocaust's enormity for Jewish American life and thought. Unlike earlier Jewish - American fiction, this literature evaluated everything. Though less successful at depicting the Holocaust experience, Jewish - American novelists successfully posed a plethora of related concerns important for both witnesses and non-witnesses, European and Jews alike. How, for example, can one imagine the unimaginable terrors of the death camps ? Theologically speaking does the covenant still exist? What find of God permitted this tragedy to engulf his chosen people? What constitutes authentic Jewish living, literature and culture ?

These are only some of the ineluctable issues confronting Jewish -American novelists.

A second generation Jewish - American literature of the Holocaust has begun to appear. The second generation phenomenon had received some psychological attention in the late 1960 s, but it was brought to public awareness with the appearance of Helen Epstein's journalistic account "Children of the Holocaust" (1979). There exists moreover a threefold red thread uniting the various expressions of Jewish - American Holocaust literature. Such literature takes seriously the search for meaning in history. Recognizes that the Holocaust is a continuing trauma both for its survivors and their children, as well as for nonwitnesses and it serves as a critique of human nature and contemporary civilization. There remains the difficulty of writing about the catastrophe of European Judaism when primary access to the event is through the imagination. But novelists can raise ultimate questions without being required to provide definitive responses. There is as well a recognition that America is increasingly the center of Jewish renewal and creativity, and its literature is, therefore distinctionly positioned to shed light on the continuing quest for authenticity in post Holocaust Jewish identity.

With the rise of Nazism in Germany and later in Austria, a new stream of Jewish immigrants arrived in the United States. Among them were a small group of highly dedicated and educated orthodox Jews. A group of orthodox Jews from Germany reorganised themselves in the Washington Heights section of New York under the leadership of Rabbi Joseph Brever (1892-1980). This group, known as Khal Adas Jeshurun, built a full scale orthodox community with a

Synagogue a school system, and a Kashruth network. This group played an important role in proving that orthodoxy could be transplanted to the United States with its strict standards intact. The most significant ideological attack against the Jews also occured during the 1920s and 1930s, it focussed not on religious issues or Jewish social climbing but on race and political subversion. A resurgent Ku Klux Klan activated the polluters. More significantly, the country witnessed the resurrection of the international stereotype of the Jew as half bankers and half Bolshevik conspiring to seize control of the nation. This belief, having been foreshadowed during the civil war, emerged in the 1980s during the Populist ferment and crystallized in the early 1920 s around auto Magnate Henry Ford. In May 1922, Ford's newspaper, the Dearborn "Independent" launched an anti- Semitic propaganda campaign without precedent in American history. It lasted for about seven years. In time, the newspaper "exposed" Jewish control of everything from the League of nations to American politics, from baseball and jazz to agriculture and movies. If any pattern of ideas activated discrimination, it was the conspiratorial ferment to which the Populists, Henry Ford and the KKK contributed.

Location of culture in Saul Bellow's The Victim:

If the Jewish writers of the thirties, as writers, failed even to survive the decade, the generation of the forties remained in its own way maudit and unfullilled and hardly acknowledged today except for its star performers. Bellow is a characteristic member of this generation, its only survivor, its only "success" as a novelist.

Bellow's heroes embody a tension between a man of love and a man of will. This can be ultimately traced to two opposing views of the world as Keith Michael Opdahl says, "Bellow is torn between his admiration of militant struggle and his insistence upon a less wilful and defenceless joy".[4] Below treats the personal and the social as a continuum in which personality finds justification in a universal principle or moral order, which it reflects, but Bellow gives a further dimension to the traditional American hero by making him embody a religious quest. Bellow's heroes seek a religious and cultural quest which distinguishes them from the protagonist's inability to break out of himself. He is unable to reconcile vision with the daily world, although he exists in a carefully defined social context. He suffers from a sense of incompletion of disunity, and yet he seeks some sort of rebirth or redemption. The world is unreal to the protagonist because he denies that he is part of it, seeking to evade limitations of physical existence, he divorces himself from it and thus divorces himself from reality. Bellow is aware of the ultimate helplessness of man before fate. He defines not the resolution of man's conflict with fate but "the very spectacle of man seeking resolution."[5]

Asa Levanthal, the protagonist of "The Victim" is caught like a helpless animal between two warring worlds of social duty and commitment to family. The family is a moral burden from the past that he has to carry on and the social duty is a kind of cross, he must bear to his own crucification. His sister-in-law is sentimental, confused and indecisive. She depends on Asa heavily for emotional and moral support, but lacks the sense of propriety. Asa is very systematically constructed as a young man without a noble family background and with an ironic suggestion i.e. history of madness in his family. His physical features, dress habits too indicate something abnormal, awkard about Asa levanthal and seen from a conventional propective, Asa is apparently unherioc. Everything in his form and stucture suggest the absence of harmony and balance and even the traditional heroic notions of handsomeness. The intention is obviously to create modern narrative prototype anti hero.

In most Jewish novels and stories, Jew is very heroic character, with few exceptions. Jew is invariably presented as victim rather than a heroic victimiser. He is not somebody set out to conquer the world or explore the limits of universe, but somebody who is conquered, constantly changed and constantly harassed. For all practical purposes, he has a very limited family. His younger brother and his wife Elena. And Asa's career as young man too is a record of failure and frustration. He takes courses in college, he cannot complete and undertakes assignments beyond his capacity and the painful feeling of doing something incompatible with his nature weighs very heavily on his heart and conscious. In no way, he is prince charming who fascinates young girls or draws attention of future employers and people who matter in business. He spends his time in reading books that are apparently outdated in the modern world. Obviously, this is an unusual and slightly ludicrous image of a hero. None the less, Asa is the centre of the narrative action.

Although critics have differed on the relationship of "The Victim" to the Holocaust, there is a general consensus that its presence is essentially muffled, if not significant. For Mark Schechner, it is "deeply hurried yet tightly woven into the fabric of the narrative, rarely explicit but always there like a symptom. L. H. Goldman notes the curious silence on the topic of Bellow's normally loquacious characters. Peter Hyland argues that despite a focus on anti- semitism, the novel does not treat the Holocaust directly, though he feels it is "haunted" by it. One of the most recent critics to dicuss the novel Michael Glenday, even rejects the importance of anti semitism to the novel. "I cannot follow the argument of those critics who regard this novel as centrally concerned with anti semitism. Glenday proceeds to a thorough revision of Allbee, who rises propotionately in the critical scale as Leventhal sinks. For Glenday, Leventhal is a "Jew" without any of the fine Jewish qualities who suffers from touchiness about anti semitism and who appears as "Caliban to Allbee's prospeor an infirma species inhabiting a "debased" reality. Glenday's view stands in strong contrast to Malcolm Bradbury's "the repulsive Allbee", Tony Tanner's "Anti Semitic" degenerate failure and Ihab Hassans refreshingly robust "insufferable creep." Apart from the discussion of anti Semitism, only one critic S. William Kremer has drawn attention to specific Holocoust material in the novel, in its pervasive images of asphyxiation, the color yellow (the badge) and closely packed trained.

In The Victim, Leventhal is away from the dreadful Holocaust. His imagery here draws upon the notion of economic disaster, but his guilt is clearly that of a survivor who did not particularly deserve to survive, but was luckier than the rest. The slippage here between economic and historical frames of reference has a special relevance to Bellow's reaction to the Holocaust. In an interview, Bellow was asked about the intellectual impact of the second world war. He replied that he had completely misunderstood the war because he was under the influence of Marxism. Although Kristall Nacht gave him pause, Bellow, as a Trotskyist, stood by the belief that a worker's state, however degenerate, could not wage an imperialist war. "I was still at that time officially sold on Marxism and revolution but sobered up when France fell." The Victim is Bellow's examination of both the guilt and the responsibilities of the survivor. It is, in a sense, about the Holocaust, because it is not ostensibly, about the Holocaust. The Victim was therapeutic for Bellow, who himself noted a change after it from gloom to holiday. Critics also have been swift to see the subsequent novel, "The Adventures of Augie March" as marking a breakthrough. Bellow's first epigraph is taken from "The tale of the Trader and the Jinni". This story is an example of the "ransom frame" in which the act of story telling serves to redeem a human life (caracciolo). In the story, the merchant is saved by the intervention of two other storytellers whose stories distract the Jinni, much as Scheherazade distracts shahriar in the frame tale from his intention to kill her. In other words, the merchant is saved from suffering as a result of a death which he did not intend, by the very process of storytelling.

As the multiple plot structures of the "Thousand and one nights" demonstate, storytelling is a better defence against the powers of death than any other, for it doubles reader, author and character by sympathetic identification a form of love. "The Victim" is a narrative of trauma which becomes a narrative of reparation, the first of a long, reparative career. Arguably, it is also highly suggestive in the paradigm offered for the importance of the theme of death in Bellow's novels and for the treatment thereof. Double plots are a common feature of Bellow's writing, with one half of the pair, as in De Quincey, often associated with the "other", America and Mexico in "the Adventures of Augie March", America and Africa in "Henderson the Rain King", America and Eastern Europe in "The Dean's December" Dr. Lal in "Mr. Sammler's Planet", Dahfu in "Henderson the Rain King, and the pickpocket in "Mr. Sammler's planet' In "Humboldt's gift", Cantabile emerges as a persecuting double when Citrine learns of the death of Humboldt, Hendreson sets off for Africa in immediate response to the death of Miss. Lenox, the death of Valeria haunts "The Dean's December". "Seize the Day" ends with Tommy Wilhelm absorbed into the crowd at a funeral. Herzog writes letters to the dead but is brought back to emotioncl health after watching the trial of a woman accused of causing the death of a small child. Even more suggestively, in the light of Bellow's ambivalence to his Trotskyite past, when Augie encounters Trotsky in Mexico, he identifies him with the power of death. "Death discredits survival is the whole success. The voice of the dead goes away. There isn't any memory. The power that's established fills the earth and destiny is whatever survives."

More generally, The Victim' offers an illuminating comparative perspective on other novels of trauma and mass death. Toni Morrison's 'Beloved', for example, with its epigraph, "Sixty million and more", focusses on the uncanny tale of a murdered child returning as a ghostly double to haunt and persecute the guilty mother, coming between mother and lover and finally being ejected only after threatening her life. Louise Erdrich's Tracks moves from an opening evocation of genocide to the resuce of a dying child and a narrative which alternates between two trickster figures, Nanapush and Pauline. As an aged Chippewa trickster figure, Nanapush may seem to have little connection to Saul Bellew's Urban heroes, yet faced with the threat of death he uses the same tactic of storytelling as survival mechanism. Asa Levanthal undergoes a great cultural conflict. In the very first chapter, when he takes the permission from Mr. Beard to go and see his sick nephew on receiving a phone call from Elena, his sister-in-law, he rudely says, "walks out right in the middle of everything Right in a pinch. With everybody else swamped"(P.3). Another voice which he identifies as that of Mr. Fay, the business manager answers, "its funny that he should just pick up and go. There must be something up" (P.3). And Mr. Beard continues, "Takes unfair advantage, like the rest of his brethren. I have never known one who wouldn't. Always please themselves first. Why didn't he offer to come back later, at least ?" (P.3)

The view of the non - Jews towards the Jews is explained through the above lines. They are not concerned about Asa's problem or his nephew's sickness, but they feel that he is taking undue advantage of becoming a Jew. Levanthal exchanges not only looks but also voices with others. In other worlds, Leventhal's consciousness mixes with those of other people around him. Asa Leventhal and his brother, Max are away from each other. There is such a difference between them that Elena, Asa's sister-in-law does not know even the name of Asa's wife, nor Philip, his nephew knows that Asa is his uncle. Bellow has very skillfully sketched the features of a typical Jew in the beginning of chapter no two. "Leventhal's figure was burly, his head large, his nose, too was large. He had black hairs, coarse waves of it, and his eyes under their intergrown brows were intensely black and of a size unusual in adult faces. But though childishly large, they were not childlike in expression. They seemed to disclose an intelligence not greatly interested in its own powers as if prefering not to be bothered by them, indifferent and this indifference appeared to be extended to others. He did not look sullen but rather unaccomodating, impassive". (P. 10).

In addition, Leventhal guesses the other's minds, he conjectures on Max's Italian-American mother-in-law's view of Mickey's rare disease in a speechless confrontation with her, Philip's state of mind, Allbee's loss of employment seem from "Rudiger's standpoint" (P.107 - 108) and Elena's view of the responsibility for Mickey's death. Mary, Asa's wife had an affair with a married man before meeting him, which disturbs Asa very much. But after Mary's persuasion, they married each other.

There is a great feeling of hatred towards the Jews, the Christians hate them vigorously. In chapter No. 3 the following lines uttered by Allbee is an example of this hatred.

"You Jews have funny ideas about drinking. Especially the one that all Gentiles are born drunkards. You have a song about it - "Drunk he is, drink he must because he is a Goy .... Schicker" (P.29) Jews often feel embarassed in the company of Christians. At Williston's house, Asa is forced to sing a Jewish song, but he feels embarassed because Allbee behaves with him in a quite different manner. Something you have really got feeling for, sing us the one about the mother. And with a drunken look of expectancy he (Allbee) bent forward, leaning on his knees, and pretended to prepare to listen. It was apparent to everyone that he was deeply pleased, he smiled at Harkarvy and the girl, and he had a glance for Leventhal too. His wife seemed quietly to dissociate herself from him. The Willistons were embarrased. Allbee was not merely an acquaintance but a friend and Williston later tried to make excuses for him and explain away the insult".

With his consciousness mixed with the other's, Leventhal comes to notice the danger of mental confinement and considers Allbee to be his "double". The others bring Leventhal not only the different views of things but also views of himself. He is brought out of mental confinement to know and build himself by the other's looks, voices and consciousness. Between Leventhal and others there exist, the conflicts of figurative looks, opinions, as well as those of literal looks. For example, Leventhal's opinions of Elena and her mother are disputed by Max. Allbee's and Leventhal's opinions are obviously in conflict with each other but whose view is true? Concerning Leventhal's view of Elena, Jonathan Baumbach writes that Bellow takes us to no discoverable final truth, only to a profound and ambiguous approximation of it. The truth is not unveiled because of the narrative structure of this novel. The extent of the narrator's information is confined to that of Leventhal as a fixed internal focalization. Therfore, there cannot be an objective judgement on whose view is the right one. Allbee has tried to validate his narrative as Leventhal's victim. However, with the disclosure of his inebriety, a probable cause of his discharge, he begins to abandon his narrative. He abandons his elitism, his ground for the superiority of WASP s. But later in the novel, he makes his place with "things as they are", or accepts or respects things as they are. Things as they are differentiates itself both from what Alibee thinks things are. They are always beyond human cognizance. Allbee remarks about Leventhal. Asa is having complex in his mind, only because he is a Jew. But though being a son of a Jew person, Philip, Asa's nephew does not know Jew language. And Allbee uses this small child to take revenge of Leventhal. This is a greatest example of Jew hatred of the WASPs.

> "Ruf mir yoshke, ruf mir JVloshke,
> Aber gib mir die groschke."

"Call me Ikey, call me Moe, but give me the dough. What's it to me if you despise me? What do you think equality with you means to me ? What do you have that I care about except the groschen?" That was Leventhal's father's view. But not his. He rejected it and recoiled from it. Anyway, his father had lived poor and died poor, that stern proud old fool with his savage looks, to whom nothing mattered save his advantage and to be freed by money from the power of his enemies. And who were the enemies. The world, everyone. They were imaginary. There was no advantage.

He carried on like a merchant prince among his bolts and remnants, and was willing to be a pack rat in order to become a lion. There was no advantage, he never became a lion. It gave Leventhal pain to think about his father's sense of these things". (P. 99)

This passage is very important in the novel, because it reflects the difference of views between Leventhal and his father. Leventhal does not want to bend before the WASPS, or any other persons due to his Jewishness, but wants to create a new culture. But his father is an oppressed one. He fears others and tells Asa also to do so. But Asa has a revolutionary mind. He fights against the injustice done to him by Allbee. "If you believe, I did it on purpose, to get even, then its not only because I am terrible personally but because I am a Jew." (P. 103) Asa understands very well that only because he is a Jew, Allbee is troubling him. "That sounds fine, Stan. But it adds up to the same thing, as far as I am concerned. You think that he burned me up and I wanted to get him in bad. Why ? Because I am a Jew; Jew are touchy, and if you hurt them they wont forgive you. That's the pound of flesh. Oh, I know you think there isn't any room in you for that, its a superstition. Every once in a while you will hear people say, "That's from the Middle Ages. "My God ! We have a name for everything, except what we really think and feel". (P. 103).

Asa knows that in American culture, Jews and their activities are given certain names. Their culture is not readily accepted by the WASPS. Asa's staunch nature and revolt against the discrimination can be clearly seen from his following words.

"What, wipe the spit off my face and leave like a gentleman ? I wouldnt think much of myself if I did." (P. 105)

The Jews in 'The Victim' are not orthodox. They are not stuck to their old traditions and customs. "Whatever comes to hand, I think. Nowadays, theater reminiscences he used to be a theatrical man. But science too, I hear. You know, I can't read Yiddish. (P.110). Harkarvy, being a Jew doesn't know Jewish language. But all the Jews are proud of their culture and their leaders. He (Disraeli) showed Europe that a Jew could be a national leader" said Goldstone. "That's Leventhal all over for you." exclaimed Harkavy. That shows you, where he stands" Jews and Empires ? Suez and India and so on ? It never seemed right to me. "You bring up Bismarck, he said. "Why did he say Jude instead of Englishman ? Disraeli was a bargainer, so he was a Jew to him, naturally."

"The Victim" reflects the modern Jewish culture where all the characters try to create a new culture but the WASPS or the anti-Jews don't allow them to do so. Asa is fighting very hard to create his own existence, but proves to be unsuccessful. The charge which Allbee puts on Asa seems fantastic when he hears it. But, it is significant that Saul Bellow persistently reminds us of Leventhal's gnawing sense of guilt. And he is finally, though grudgingly, forced to assume responsibility. He asks, I haven't thought about you in years, frankly, and I don't know why you think I care whether you exist or not. What, are we related ?"

"By blood ?No.. Heavens" (P. 29) answers Allbee. The theme is thus explicitly stated: how man is related to man, not by blood, of Jew to Jew but as man caught in the tangled web of social reality. The force of the conviction however, does not rest so much on the apparent justice of Allbee's complaint as in the convert intimidations with which he often frequents Leventhal's house rappealing for sympathy and gradually Leventhal gives him almost everything he asks, for money to tide over his difficulties and bed in his apartment. Allbee consciously reminds him of the fate which Levanthal secretly believes is his, insistently identifying Leventhal "a deep Hebrew" with the racial characteristics of "his people", implying thereby that Jew is outside the human community, a community to which this degraded, drifting alcoholic, a gentile really belongs.

In the Jewish culture in "The Victim", the paradox of anti semitism in which the Jew is forced to be more than others and is actually accused of betraying human values precisely by those who are inhumanly treating him is thus articulated. The novel exposes the Jew's own sense of guilt, for Levanthal is both the victim and the victimiser. He seems unwilling to accept his own responsibility as an integral part of his destiny as a human being. This becomes obvious from his last chance meeting with Allbee.

Thus, the development of Bellow's hero is from alienation to accommodation from denial to acceptance. This accommodation as Marcus Klein has averred "has meant in all cases an impossible reconciliation, a learning to live with, and at the same time, a learning to deny. What has been plainly there.". The Bellow hero confronts a strong sense of self, the sacrifice of self demanded by social circumstances and finally learns to humble himself in the intricate texture of reality. As Ihab Hassan has observed if "they (Bellow's heroes) ends with humility, they begin in humiliation.

Location of culture in I. B. Singer's "Shosha"

Study of Yiddish literature, however reveals the classical Yiddish literary tradition itself is not predominately one of prettification, that the sores and boils which afflicted East European Jewish life were plainly evident to the older writers and were unabashedly treated in their literary works. The observation that Isaac Bashevis Singer frequently presents Jews in "a bad light' is certainly accurate. But the same accusation could be made against I. L. Peretz, Sholem Asch, I. J. Singer, certainly Mendele Moykher Sforim, and even Sholem Aleichem. Nevertheless, however vaguely they perceive this, Singer does in fact represent a significant deviation from the tradition of Yiddish literature which more Yiddish readers accept and into which they except modern Yiddish works to fit.

In lamenting his enforced exile from Germany and his consequent loss of contact with the German public, Thomas Mann once described his books as the product of a reciprocal educational bond between nation and author, depending on shared assumptions which the author himself has helped to create. Such a description can nowhere more accurately be applied than to the works of the older generation of Yiddish writers. Mendele Moykher Sforim, Sholem Aleichem and I. L. Peretz, the triad of "classical" Yiddish writers, display considerable and significant differences from one another with respect to theme, style and literary attitude. But they were all in the first instance social writers. That is to say, they viewed their writing directly in the context of the audience for whom they wrote. Mendele describes the inner struggle which precede his division to brave ridicule by writing in the despised Yiddish tongue, instead of in Hebrew as previously. The struggle was resolved when he asked himself, "For whom am I working?" And the answer came in this form. "Let come what will, I will take pity on the Yiddish language, that outcast daughter. It is time to do something for the people." Sholem Aleichem refers to himself repeatedly as a folksshrayber a writer of (for) the people, while one of Peretz's little known criticisms of Sholem Aleichem rests on the view that the latter "doesn't do things, doesn't call on people to do things - he laughs. And makes us laugh".

This does not mean that classical Yiddish literature was necessarily programmatic Mendele's work is openly tendentious, at first frankly preaching the message of enlightenment, a message whose inadequacy to the problem was progressively illuminated, even to the author himself, by the very fidelity and clarity with which Mendele Peretz nor Sholem Alichem promotes a particular program in his writing, yet their works, with all of the patent differences between them, share certain characteristics which are also to be found in those of Mendele. Central to the similarity is the view that the shtetl life of nineteenth century East European Jewry needed to be changed drastically, and the conviction that reform and progress were not only essential, but also possible. Mendele is unsparing in his castigation of Jewish civic leaders for their greed, ignorance and complacency. Peretz writes scathingly of "dead towns" and Sholem Aleichem begs the reader not to be offended that he speaks such harsh words to his Kasrilevke people, I am, you understand, my dear friends, myself a Kasrilevker". Common to all three writers, and of greater importance than the element of social criticism which is evident in these examples, is the assumption that the writer's function included the obligation to reproach, admonish, cajole and encourage his readers. And this assumption was shared by the readers who valued "their" writers partly in proportion to their efficacy as teachers.

It is not clear to what extent the classicists actually believed that their visions of Jewish community would be achieved. There is nevertheless implicit in traditional yiddish literature the rationalist conviction that improvement was possible, that social controls could be imposed, and that the forces of cohesion could be made to previal. These forces were regarded as fundamental, no matter how weak they had become, while the shocking conditions which the writers angrily exposed, even if predominant, were viewed as symptoms and consequences of the aberrant breakdown of social order. The founders were not only rationalist, but also, whatever their personal religious convictions, essentially secular writers. Their central literary concentration was upon "the Jewish question" and this meant for them, without exception, the question of the Jew in the modern world. None of them conceived of a Jewish solution in any sort of withdrawal from the world. As secular writers to be sure, they reflected the concerns of only a segment of the Yiddish speaking population. Chassidim, for example did not read Yiddish literature on principle for worldly literature was to them at worst treyf and at best trivial. Other segments of the population, particularly some varieties of Zionists, rejected Yiddish literature not for its secular orientation but for its use of the despised Yiddish" Zhargon" as a literary vehicle. Nevertheless, a broad range of readers coming largely from the working and middle classes was secured. And the equally fervent commitment of the founders to communal integrity and to social justice made it possible for readers at every point of a spectrum ranging from class. Conscious workers to comfortable petit. Commercants to find in traditional Yiddish literature their cultural sustenance and an echo of their own shtetl experiences.

The shtetl of Isaac Bashevis singer is at once both reminiscent of and strangely different from that of the Yiddish classicists. It has often been remarked that the body of traditional Yiddish literature offers so clear and detailed a picture of shtetl culture that it can serve virtually as a source of ethnographic data. To the insider, the reader who himself emerged from it, it is instantly recognizable. The outsider, on the other hand, requires elaborate explanations or at least a glossary, to orient himself in the environment. Singer's shtetl presents largely the same landmarks. Yet, it is unacknowledged by most remaining shtetl immigrants, while readers from "outside appear to find their way about easily. Neither the motivations of Singer's characters nor their destinies are dependent on the specific cultural content of shtetl existence.

His primary concern is with the perpetual struggle between good and evil for the soul of man, a struggle which goes on constantly, and primarily on a plane of human existence which has little to do with the rational. The physical as well as the cultural environment are important only as a viewing device through which the immanent struggle becomes manifest in dimensions which are temporally and spatially definable. The shtetl of the classicists is primarily comprehensible in terms of the social community which it represents or aspires to become. The shtetl of Singer is not a community at all. It is a society in disarray Singers shtetl is the locus in nuce of the anomie which he sees as endemic to the condition of the world.

Singer's modernism as a Yiddish author consists in the fact that his concern is not primarily with the "Jewish question" but rather with the human condition, and moreover that those aspects of humanity which are to him most fascinating are the non rational. His style is vividly realistic and this makes even more striking the impression, objectionable to many traditional Yiddish readers, that to the author a succubus and a Yeshiva bokher are equally real. Traditional Yiddish literature did not exclude the occult.

Faithful recorders that they were, the founders described many elements of folk belief in their works. Blessings, curses, spirits, charms to ward off the evil eye, and the like. But these were always identified as superstition as symptoms of backwardness, and were treated with ridicule or condescension.

Preservation of old Jewish values has always been one of the major themes of Singerian fiction. Shosha and her mother still observe the faith and carry on the ancient traditons. It is this innocence that makes Aaron to forsake his chance to marry Betty and leave for America before the Nazi invasion. In the realist setting of this novel, Singer shows a sensitive, thoughtful individual caught between contending drives. In Shosha, the first chapter opens with the lines, "I was brought up on three dead languages. Hebrew, Aramaic and Yiddish (some consider the last not a language at all) and in a culture that developed in Babaylon. The Talmud the Cheder where I studied was a room in which the teacher ate and slept, and his wife cooked. There, I studied not arithmatic, geography, physics, chemistry or history, but the laws governing an egg laid on a holiday and sacrifices in a temple destroyed two thousand years ago. Although my ancestors had settled in Poland some six or seven hundred years before I was born, I knew only a few words of the Polish language. We lived in Warsaw on Krochmalna street, which might well have been called a ghetto. Actually the Jews of Russian occupied Poland were free to live wherever they chose. It was an anachronism in every way, but I didn't know it, just as I didnt know that my friendship with Shosha, the daughter of our neighbour Bashele and her husband Zelig had anything to do with love !" (P.3)

These lines reflect that this piece of fiction is written by a person who is a traditional Jew. Isaac Bashevis Singer is a traditional Jew person who has reflected all the Jewish traditions and customs in Shosha. His awareness of being Jewish is very strong. Jewish philosophy about life and life after death is depicted in the novel. It is very important to note that, this philosophy is given by a rabbi. The Jews are not beautiful, rather they are ugly. This is a great misunderstanding throughout the world. Aaron, the protagonist, as a child was singled out in particular because he was a rabbis son and wore a long gaberdine and a velvet cap. The boys taunted him with names like "Fancypants, little Rabbi, Mollycoddle." If they heard him speaking to Shosha, they jeered and called him "Sissy." He was also teased for having red hair, blue eyes and unusually white skin. (P.6).

The second world war has a great impact on the Jewish culture. The smooth life of the Jews was totally disturbed by this unwanted event. Singer has given the worse conditions that followed after the war. "At home we soon began to go hungry. In the time between the assassination in Sarajevo and the outbreak of the war, many wealthy housewives had stocked their larders with flour, rice, beans and groats, but my mother had been busy reading morality books. Besides, we had no money. The Jews on our street stopped paying my father. There were no more weddings, divorces or lawsuits in his courtoom. Long lines formed at the bakeries for a loaf of bread. The prize of meat soared. In Yanash's Bazaar the slaughterers stood with knives in their hands looking out for a woman with a chicken, a duck, or a goose." (P. 12) After the world war, it became very difficult for the Jews to follow their culture and their traditions. They were put in rehabilitation camps. Aaron was also put in such type of a camp, but he was not sure that his Jewish purity will be protected there. Aaron faced a great blow on his religion, spirituality and also on culture. Being a son of a rabbi and a true Jew, he was strictly brought up on the traditional Jewish rituals, but the world war made him suffer the worst things in his life. With the German soldiers enlightenment had invaded Krochmalna street. Aaron had heard of Darwin and was no longer sure that the miracles described in "The Assembly of Saints" had really occured. Ever since war had broken out on the Ninth Day of Ab, the Yiddish newspaper was brought daily into our house and he read about Zionism, Socialism and following the Russian evacuation of Poland when the Russian censorship ceased a series of articles about Rasputin. After the world war his world changed and he was slowly moving away from the Jewish culture.

The threat of second world war was always on the Jews. The newspapers talked of how modern the German army had become, fully mobilized and equipped with the latest weapons, but the Polish soldiers looked just like the Russian soldiers in 1914. They wore heavy greatcoats and the sweat poured from their faces. Their rifles appeared too long and too bulky. All of them were doomed to be massacred, yet they made fun of the Jews in the long gaberdines. One even tugged at a Jews beard, and they could be heard hissing "Zydy, Zydy, Zydy". (P.67). When Aaron was travelling with Betty and Sam, he saw this cruel picture. In Germany, Hitler had solidified his power, but the Warsaw Jews were so strong about their culture that they celebrated the festival of the exodus out of Egypt four thousand years ago. Aaron was also strict about Jewish culture, when Betty brought a bouquet for him and Tekla, his maid servant put it in a vase, he was very surprised, because he had never heard of woman bringing flowers for a man. Fietelzohn as a Jew gives the simple principle of humanity which most of the human beings don't follow. He says that the basis of ethics is man's right to play the game of his choice. I will not trample on your toys and you will not trample on mine. I wont spit on your idol and you will not spit on mine. There is no reason why hedonism the Cabala, polygamy, ascetism, even our friend Haiml's blend of eroticism and Hasidism could not exist in a playcity or play world a sort of a Universal coney Island where everyone would play according to his or her own desire." (P.135)

The Kabbalah which simply means "tradition" is a collective term for a variety of esoteric teachings based on the Torah and developed for generations by Jewish mystics. Singer uses the religious thought of the ancient Kabbalah to explore the godless vision of the Modern world and in doing so, he maintains in his fiction a precarious balance between the biblical and the secular between belief & disbelief. Beneath the surface of simple "folktale", "Shosha", an elaborate process is seen wherein the dynamics of fiction are tightly joined with the assumptions of faith and culture. Singer, in the most modern of manner, manipulates fictional conventions to further his thematic considerations and posits a new transcendence based, not upon the supernatural, but upon the infinite possibilities of language and the imagination. Storytelling itself is a motif which runs throughout the fiction. Singer's fiction overflows with a cacophony of narratives voices- whispering gossiping, sharing secret stories. In tales with contemporary settings, narrators, in varying degrees rather closely resembling the author himself, are writers of note who share stories with us or are pursued by those obsessed with sharing theirs.

For Singer, storytelling is a significant action, rooted in the primal act of creation and associated with the linguistic theories of the Kabbalah. Often he makes playful allusions to these association. In "Shosha" the life of the Jews during and after the war is shown. "Shosha" traces the characteristic motions of human destiny, a heavy climb upward, a rapid tumble downward. Life forms a journeying to heaven and hell, mostly hell. What determines the direction a man will take ? Sometimes the delicate maneouvres between his will and desire, sometimes the heat of his vanity, sometimes the blessings of innocence. But more often than not, it is all mystery which Singer chooses to present rather than explain. As his figures move upward and downward, aflame with the passion of their ineluctable destiny, they stop for a moment in the shtetl world. Singer is not content with the limitations of materiality, yet not at all indifferent to the charms and powers of the phenomenal Universe.

The historical settings of East European Jewish life are richly presented in "Shosha", often not as orderly sequences in time but as simultaneous perceptions jumbled together in the consciousness of figures. It is hardly a secret that in the Yiddish literary world, Singer is regarded with certain suspicion. Within his limits, Singer is a genius. He has total command of his imagined wor'd, he is original in his use both of traditional Jewish materials and his modernist attitude towards them, he provides a serious if enigmatic moral perspective and he is a master of yiddish prose. To this buried strand of Jewish experience Singer has been drawn in fascination and repulsion, potraying its manifestations with great vividness and its consequences with stern judgement. It is a kind of experience that rarely figures in traditional yiddish writing, yet is a significant aspect of the Jewish past. Bringing this material to contemporary readers, Singer writes in Yiddish but often quite apart from the Yiddish tradition, indeed, he is one of the few Yiddish writers whose relation to the Jewish past is not determined or screened by that body of values we call Yiddishism.

Institutional discrimination against Jews in housing and employment was sharply reduced. Jews began to enjoy greater political success. Jews were elected to the congress, the Senate and other high political offices in numbers far disproportionate to the size of the Jewish population. In the 101st congress sworn in on January 3, 1989 there were 31 Jewish members of ttn House of Representatives and 8 Jewish Senators, one of whom is believed to be the first orthodox Jew elected to the chamber. By the 1980s, some would feel that anti semitism in the United states, once a serious problem, was a thing of past.

Kaplan was first to observe that the Jewish crisis of modernity is a direct result and the loss of social and cultural cricumstances. Socially, since the beginning of 19th century, Jews in various places have undergone political emancipation that has granted them citizenship as individuals in their nations of residence. They participate fully in the surrounding and thus now have a choice their ancestors lacked about whether and how to identify and participate as Jews. For Jewish civilization to thrive in the modern world, Kaplan believed that the traditional pre-emancipation community would have to be reconstituted. He proposed and advocated the formation of an organic community, a super Kehillah to nurture the development of functioning Jewish communities in North America. The community which Jews would join by payment of dues, would include all religious and secular Jewish organizations and would have a monopoly on providing Jewish services, life cycle rituals, Kosher food, worship services, and social and educational programs.

Notes:

1. Kazin Alfred ; "Though he slay me" P. no.3.
2. Doctorow E. L.: "The Book of Daniel" Pub (1971).
3. Bhabha K.Homi P. no. 1.
   The Location of culture: London and New York.
4. Dickstein Morris: Cold war Blues Partisan Review Vol. XLI year - 1974. Pg. no. 30.
5. Bellow Saul: The Victim 1947, London Alison Press, 1984.

Glossary:

1. Dybbuk - a condemned spirit who inhabits the body of a living person and controls his or her actions.
2. Galut - exile, condition of Jewish people in exile.
3. Gemarah - section of the Talmud interpreting the mishnah.
4. Goy - a gentile, a non-Jew, literally Hebrew for "nation".

5. Halakhah - that part of Jewish literature which deals with religious, ethical, civil and criminal law.

6. Hasidim - religous, enthusiasts, devotees of Hasidim or "pietism", a religious revival beginning in the 18th century.

7. Mishnah - earliest codification of the oral law, which is the basis of the Talmud.

8. Sefirot - literally "numbers" in Hebrew, plural form of sefira, Cabalistic term for emanations and manifestatios of the godhead.

9. Shechinah - divine presence.

10. Shevuot - teast of the Pentecost, festival commemorating the giving of the Torah to Moses.

11. Shtetl - Jewish town or village of Eastern Europe.

12. Talmud - result and record of eight centuries of study and discussion of the Bible by Jewish scholars in the academies of Palestine and Babylonia.

13. Torah - narrowly, the Pentateuch, but by extension all Jewish teaching.

14. Yeshiva - institute for higher learning in Judasim.

15. Kosher - ritual for preparing food.

BIBLIOGRAPHY

Primary Sources:

1. Bhabha K. Homi: "The Location of Culture", London and New York. 1988.

2. Bellow Saul: "The Victim": 1947. Pengiun Books 1996.
3. Singer I. B.: "Shosha": New York: Farrar Straus and Giroux, 1978, published serially in Yiddish in the Forward in 1974.
4. Kaplan Mordecai M.: Judaism as a civilization New York: Schocken, 1934.

Secondary Sources:

1. Allen Tate, "Techniques Of Fiction", The Man Of Letters In The Modern world (New York, 1955).
2. Alexander, Edward. "Isaac Bashevis Singer" Boston: Twayne Publishers, 1980.
3. Albert, Rebecca T. and Staub, Jacob J. Exploring Judaism. A Reconstructionist Approach. New York; 1985
4. Bradbury, Malcolm"Saul Bellow". London: Methuen, 1982.
5. Bernstein Saul: The Renaissance of the Torah Jew Hoboken, N. J. Ktav 1985.
6. Borkin Joseph: The Crime and Punishment of I. G. Farben. The Birth., Growth and Corruption of a Giant corporation, London, Andre Deutsch, 1979.
7. Barrell, John. "The infection of Thomas De Quincey; A Pgychopathology of Imperialism". New Haven and London: Yale UP, 1991.
8. Buchen, Irving, "Isaac Bashevis Singer And The Eternal Past", New York: New York University Press, 1968.

9. Caracciolo Peter L. (ed), The Arabian Nights in English Literature: Studies in the Reception of the Thousand and one Night into British culture: London: Macmillan, 1988.

10. Coates Paul. "The Double And The Other: Identity As Ideology In Post-Romantic Faction. London: Macmillan, 1988,

11. De Quincey, Thomas. "Confessions Of An English OpiumEater: Ed. Richard Garnett. London: Kegan Paul, Trench, Trubner, 1891.

12. Davis, Moshe. The Emergence of Conservative Judaism. Philadelphia; Jewish Publication Society, 1963.

13. Dorff, Elliot N. Conservative Judaism: Our Ancestors To Our Descendants. New York; United Synagogue of America, 1977.

14. Diamond, Sander The Nazi Movement in the United States: 1924-1971. Ithaca N.Y. Cornell University Press, 1974.

15. Epstein, Helen "Children Of The Holocaustt" New York: G. P. Putnam's Sons, 1979.

16. Erdrich, Louise. Tracks London: Picador 1989.

17. Eisenstein, Ira. Judaism Under Freedom. New York: Reconstructionist Press, 1956.

18. Ed. Jack Fischel and Sanford Pinsker, Jewish American History and culture; An Encyclopedia. Vol.429. 1980.

19. Fuchs Daniel: Saul Bellow: Vision and Revision: Durham ; Duke U. P. 1984.

20. Freud, Sigmund. The Uncanny". The Standard Edition Of The Complete Psychological works of

Sigmund Freud. Vol. XVII. Ed. James Strachey London: Hogarth Press, 1955. 219- 52.

21. Goldman, L. H. "The Jewish Perspective of Saul Bellow" Ed. L. H. Goldman, Gloria Cronin and Ada Aharoni: "Saul Bellow A Mosaic", New York: Peter Long, 1992.

22. Glenday, Michael. "Saul Bellow And The Decline Of Humanism" London: Macmillan, 1990.

23. Gordon, Milton M.Assimilation in American Life. New York; Oxford University Press, 1964.

24. Green, Arthur, See My Face. Speak My Name: A Contemporary Jewish Theology In Press:

25. "Howe Irving: "I. B. Singer": Yiddish Tradition vs. Jewish Tradition: A Dialogue" Midstream 19 (June) (July 1975).

26. Ihab Hassan 'Saul Bellow: Five Faces Of A Hero', Critique vol. III (New York, 1966).

27. Jonathan Baumback: The Landscape of Nightmare (New York 1965).

28. Kaufman, Jonathan: Broken Alliance: New York. Scribner, 1988.

29. Keith Michael Opdahal "The Novels of Saul Bellow: An Introduction (The Pennsylvani a State University, 1967).

30. Kresh, Paul. "Isaac Bashevis, Singer". New York: Dial Press, 1979.

31. Klein, Isaac. A Guide to Jewish Religious Practice, New York; Jewish Theological Seminary 1979. Reconstructionist Press, 1985.

32. The Meaning of God In Modern Jewish Religion New York: Behrman House, 1937.

33. Zatlin, Linda G. "The Themes of Isaac Bashevis Singer's Short Fiction". Critique (1969).

INTERVIEWS

1. Andersen David M. "Isaac Bashevis Singer: Conversations In California" Modern fiction studies 16 (winter 1970-71)

2. Blocker, Joel and Richard Elman. "An Interview with Isaac Bashevis Singer" Commentary 36 (November 1963).

3. Burgin, Richard, and Isaac Bashevis Singer. "Conversations with Isaac Basahavis Singer. New York; Doubleday, 1985.

4. Gilman, Sander L. "Interview / Isaac Dashevis Singer" Diacrictis 4 (Spring 1974)

5. Lee, Grace Farrell "Stewed Prunes and Rice Pudding: College students Eat and Talk with Isaac Bashevis Singer. "Contemporary literature 19 (Autumn 1978).

6. Pinsker, Sanford. "Isaac Bashevis Singer: An Interview". Critique" (1969).

7. Ribalow, Reen Sara. "A visit to Isaac Bashevis Singer". "The Reconstructionist 30 (29th May 1964).

8. Rosenblatl Paul and Gene Koppel. "Isaac Bashevis Singer on Literature and life" Tueson: University of Arizona Press, 1971.